Poised In Flight

Edited by: A.J. Huffman
and April Salzano

Cover Art by A.J. Huffman

Copyright © 2013 A.J. Huffman

All rights reserved. Except for brief quotations in critical articles or reviews, no part of this book may be reproduced in any manner without prior written permission from the publisher:

Kind of a Hurricane Press
www.kindofahurricanepress.com
kindofahurricanepress@gmail.com

CONTENTS

April Salzano	**Intro:** *Airplanes, Angels and Abstractions*	3
	From The Poets	
Ken Adler	*When I Was Fifteen*	7
Joe Amaral	*Immigrant Egret*	9
	Breakfast Cranny	10
	The Window Seat	11
Linda Bearss	*Flying on a Gold Wing*	13
Alan Britt	*This Time the Clouds*	14
	Poem Written on a Summer Evening in Maryland	15
Terry Brix	*A Mild Breeze – When Anvils Fly*	16
	Flights to Oblivion	17
Diana Brodie	*About a Brother*	18
Michael H. Brownstein	*The Color of Sound in the City*	20
Dorothy Burgess	*The Moth*	21
Janet Butler	*Icarus*	22
Miki Byrne	*The Visitor*	23
Tiffany Chaney	*The Mind is a Bird's Nest*	24
Esteban Colon	*Wax in the Sunshine*	26
	Beyond Blinds	27

	The Bird	29
Susan Dale	*My Homing Pigeon Heart*	30
	Of Time	32
Cassandra Dallett	*Losing Feathers*	33
Jim Davis	*Potential*	35
	Fruitfly	36
R.C. Davis	*Tread Mark Upon Airborne Cloud*	38
Neil Ellman	*Metamorphosis*	40
Alexis Rhone Fancher	*Flight (haiku series)*	41
Mike Florian	*Winds Calm and Variable*	43
Patricia L. Goodman	*Sex in Midair*	45
	Cold Hope	46
	Flipping Grief the Bird	48
Mavis Gulliver	*Invocation*	49
Nels Hanson	*Eucalyptus*	50
Richard D. Hartwell	*Full Light*	52
Art Heifetz	*A Dream of Flight*	53
S. E. Ingraham	*When Angels Fly Too Close*	55
	Anticipating Rionero and the Swallows	57
	Humbling Journeys	58

Ken L. Jones	The Feathered Poet	59
Lora Keller	Will	60
	What Remains	61
	Your Best Bow	62
Steve Klepetar	Empire of Trees	64
Len Kuntz	On the Wing	65
Heller Levinson	Flute Carved from the Wing Bone of a Red Crowned Crane	67
	Mongolian Eagle's Ascent	69
pd lyons	Morgan's Birds	74
Jacqueline Markowski	Intelligent Design	75
Joe Massingham	King Fisher	76
	The Hawk	77
Janet McCann	Look Homeward, Thomas	78
Joan McNerney	Wildflowers	79
Karla Linn Merrifield	Another Message from a Harpy Eagle	80
	At the Amazon Avian Checklist Station	81
	Feathered Friend Fibonacci	82
Bradley Morewood	Morning Song	83
	3112 Archipelago Lane	84

Heidi Morrell	Winged	85
Lylanne Musselman	Bird Lessons	86
Robbi Nester	Memory	88
	Newcomers	89
	The Sibyl to Her Fowl	90
ayaz daryl nielsen	Peregrine	91
	Fruitfly	92
Alex Nodopaka	Wings of Immortality	93
Selena Parrish	Two Dogs Chained	95
Winston H. Plowes	White Vessel with Inverted Triangle	96
PratimaBalabhadrapathruni	Légende	97
	Nervous Anticipation	98
Ben Rasnic	Prayer	99
henry 7. reneau, jr.	The Price of Flight	101
	Red	103
	An Extraordinary Machine	105
Sy Roth	13 Miles to Somewhere	106
Walter Ruhlmann	PMT3 -- August 2010	107
	A Wing Can Cover All Sorts of Things	108
Elizabeth Schultz	Hummingbird in the Bookstore	110
	Mosquito Obsession	111

	Romance	112
Lance Sheridan and Barbara Sutton	*She Swung Forth to Find the Fall of Night*	113
Carol Smallwood	*Smoke from Burning Leaves*	114
Edward W. L. Smith	*A Murder of Crows*	115
Shelby Stephenson	*A Walnut Falls on the Tin Roof of the Mule Stable*	118
John Swain	*Also Watched*	120
	On the Reed Stalks	121
Susan Tepper	*Air Over Hanoi*	122
Anca Vlasopolos	*Calls to Passage*	126
Mercedes Webb-Pullman	*To My Father*	127
Laura Grace Weldon	*Why the Window Washer Reads Poetry*	129
	So Soon	130
Sara Williams	*Above All Else*	131
Martin Willitts, Jr.	*Return Flight*	132
	Finding the Blue Huron	134
	Sidemen or Birds on the Same Wave Length Branch	135
Juliet Wilson	*The Weaver Bird Colony*	140
Diana Woodcock	*Together We Watch*	141
	Migrations	142

Abigail Wyatt	*The Late Blooming of Harriet Milne*	144
Dana Yost	*A Light of Their Own*	147
Ed Zahniser	*September 29, Altitude 30,000 Feet*	148
Ali Znaidi	*What I Learned from the Flying Wings*	149

From The Editors

A.J. Huffman	*Poised in Flight*	153
	The Fire Catches	154
	Of Perch and Purpose	155
	From Balloon This Eruption	156
	Have a Happy Period	157
April Salzano	*Footless Pigeons*	158
	Layovers	159
	Summoning Seagulls	160
	Flying South	162
	Auto Pilot	163
	Author Bios	167
	About the Editors	187

Airplanes, Angels and Abstractions

Initially, we were both elated and overwhelmed by the sheer volume of submissions for this anthology. Every day brought in dozens more flight poems. Once we began the selection process, we quickly realized the quality of the work we had received was among our best, featuring writing from previous contributors as well as authors we had not heard from before. While this made our job no easier, it certainly made it enjoyable. Unfortunately, our task included eliminating some fine pieces for such minor reasons as avoiding redundancy on particular subtopics. We thank each artist who submitted and encourage them all to continue doing so, not only to our journals and anthologies, but to the many other small presses that seek to give writers a place to share their art.

We have spent the past weeks communicating across our respective climates to choose the best poems and flash fiction to offer our readers on one of our favorite themes, "wings." As with previous anthologies, our vision was to offer a thorough yet distinctive examination of what a particular concept means to contemporary writers. Our authors took flight across meadows and memories, clouds and metaphors, on the wings of birds, airplanes and mythology. Collectively, the art here follows a diverse path to conveying these unique interpretations of theme through a wide range of styles and voices. Our authors provided representations of form and free verse, traditional and abstract. Their speakers watch birds in flight with wonder and astonishment, showing reverence for nature and its ability to humble us. Wings become metaphor for tools needed to live among our fellow humans, for failed attempts to understand each other's emotions, for fear and freedom, and as a vehicle by which to delve into the depths of the psyche. Wings also provide a height from which we can observe the world below with a new perspective. Time is often suspended or rendered irrelevant, however briefly, when speakers and subjects take to the skies. At times, bodies sprout wings for reasons equally diverse: to escape, to remember, to leave, to return.

In the pages of our latest anthology, these pieces will take readers on a journey more intense and eclectic than we had anticipated. We hope everyone enjoys the ride as much as we have!

From The Poets

When I Was Fifteen

My dad and I did not see eye to eye.
Me: long hair, bell-bottom pants, and paisley shirts.
He, dressed like Joey Bishop, drank Martinis after work.
I played guitar, sang Beatle songs, and sighed.
Flower Power versus Happy Hour.
Still, I got to fly

in the co-pilot seat to Hollywood one time. We flew
south along the Rockies to a place
we could get through, the light in my face,
the blue wall between us
and our goal. We knew
the drone of the engine, constant.

Monument Valley's strange sandstone chimneys
and The Painted Desert slipped by below.
Headwinds made the going slow.
Thermals had us pitch and lurch.
Crackling radio, spirit voices speaking Pilotese,
the drone of the engine, constant.

With maps unfolded across my knees
I scanned for landmark icons.
Then, on the horizon, the Grand Canyon
spread out like a lizard in the sun.
As we drew near, the depth became apparent.
The engine coughed, and sputtered. The drone went silent.

Suspended, quiet above that hole,
now twice as high as moments ago,
we hung out together, over the edge, peering down.
Dad told me later, on firmer ground,

that he had not been certain
we would make it.

                   -- Ken Adler

Immigrant Egret

There sits in the slits
between spots where
concrete and shrub merge

The last unicorn

Glistening knight white, a
real life myth carving out
a niche in the crawlspace

Ignoring the truck thunder
scattering litter, minutemen
poisoning the marsh

One leg poised in
hunter stance, searching for
yellow-orange beaks,
a tattered sunray, burning flags

You may wonder how
wide, low-slung wings
can hover over the rigs
at rush hour (they can't)

So you hope there is
patience enough to wait
for darkness to quell traffic

Or when the coyotes howl
Survival depends on the innate
ability to sneak over
and under manmade barriers.

-- Joe Amaral

Breakfast Cranny

We escape the clutches of dawn
Her icy chill casting our bones in cement
Strolling into a bagel café
Ordering croissants and coffee

A tiny songbird flutters indoors
Banging her head against the window
Continuously astir in aggravation
Do something! You plead aghast

Everyone else just stares
Some even snicker as I rise
Pausing to gaze at the poor creature
Twittering in trapped terror

I thrust my hands out quick
Capturing beating wings and heart
I feel a warm shudder, defeated supplication
Then amble outside to astonishing gasps

The rind of sunlight glitters cold
But the blue sky shows a summer noon
I open my soft grip, a hatchling in flight
Letting the songbird take off like a musical note

Chirping free in the frisky air

-- Joe Amaral

The Window Seat

What lies beneath her
folded brow and
bent brain? Faraway eyes
mutely gazing into

Sky blue oblivion

Where teardrops carve
fissures down her face like
glistening icicles
dying in sunlight

Waterfalls of blue

This stranger sitting nearby
on a fated overseas flight
I dare not speak to her
The ignorance is mutual

Floating bluely adrift

For twelve hours we shift
in epic silence
The seeds of friendship
unplanted, unsown

Darkling blue hearts

Locked away in our own
selfish worlds
We guard our intimacy in
jealous suspicion

Fear is blue

Watching with hooded eyes
frozen in time, never
viewing what lies beneath
the masked, mystic clouds

Blue thunderstorms

Her eyes close,
her tears dry, wraithlike
she ghosts past me
disappearing down the aisle

Forever blue

                      -- Joe Amaral

Flying on a Gold Wing

"It's freedom," he said, weathered face and dimples,
smiling like a boy with his first engine, first solo on the road.

"Watch the curve," I plead.

I feel loose like a puppet whose strings are cut,
hands gripping the cold, chrome bars, trying
to stabilize arms that want to reach frantically
for support where there is none, never enough
to stop my flesh from grinding into the pavement.

"Don't lean the bike so close to the pavement," I beg.

I hold onto his torso, broad back, zippered black leather.
He smells like Chrome cologne – my eyes close,
knowing I mustn't lean away from the turn,
fighting primitive instincts, self-preservation 101.
With each curve the asphalt climbs,
threatening to chew my chaps and shred my skin.
The threats choke, hollow echoes fading with the landscape.

I choose to hang on to learn to share his passion, to taste
his joy in the freedom to risk it all – the freeway rises as our
runway.

Resolved, I force open my eyes, spread my arms,
shedding my fear of flying in one great exhalation.
I soar with him; we embrace and ride the rushing wind.

-- Linda Bearss

This Time the Clouds
(for Ultra Violet)

This time the clouds
rub their hips
against the branches of our thoughts.

Dried leaves tumble
to the blacktop covered
by redyellow ashes.

Clouds on ice-skates
circle these leaves,
darkening our thoughts,
stirring our imaginations.

-- Alan Britt

Poem Written on a Summer Evening in Maryland

This blank page,
a dirty white feather
discarded
by mute swan
against
smooth
soapstone.

At sunrise,
the swan's shadow
glides
across shallow
brackish bay water.

Currents of death
flowing
through
the swan's webbed feet
caress
a mourning dove's
crushed trumpet.

-- Alan Britt

A Mild Breeze – When Anvils Fly

The wind is strong today in Havre, Montana.
Anvils fly past like meteors,
horseshoes like motes of dust.
If the jet stream speed continues until tomorrow,

I'll be able to pick up sniffs of Christian Dior's
latest panel sniff-tested musk perfume for the Paris fall,
get a hint of radon decay from the most recent Russian
incident over Siberia as my thyroid shutters,
scoop up the smell of Peking duck, and soy and
deep-thrusted Oriental love making,
sense the last gasp of a California writer we don't know today
but will after we read him when he is dead,
pick out your scent from the olfactory static of millions of women
this wind has picked over for friendly smells.

Hidden in those massive chunks of air that can twirl counties,
I smell you near me even though you are a world wind
circumference away.
Nothing actually to do with the wind bringing you to me.
Just love and your scent finding me
in a mild breeze when anvils fly.

-- Terry Brix

Flights to Oblivion

Finland's Helsinki Klaus Kurki bar posted drink prices on the wall
like airport flight departures where I could imagine my escape routes.
The booze of choice is the initial taste destination,
the price is the gate to get in and to get seated.

But actually the destination is the same; traffic control, my control, is a sham.
They are all flights to oblivion three, five, ten drinks away.
I sit and stare at the flight board and wish I could fly:

>Billies Booch sounds like a female organ to me,
>a Woodpecker after all that booze I doubt,
>Dirty Imagination sounds enticingly anal,
>the Leg Spreader positively irresistible.

But my new flights are to anywhere not on the board, cost nothing, and
you never actually arrive but are a work in progress.

-- Terry Brix

About a Brother

I   *Daedalus dreams the pattern of wings*

'Find soft breast feathers of a swan that sings.
Force down the fiery fly-past of a parrot's wings.
Sew these plumes together. Now thwart a peacock's pride.
His haughtiness is his downfall. Flaunt his feathers on both sides.
Reach high for a prize from eagle. For humming bird, stoop low.
But the gods seek vengeance, though, for hubris. Be cunning here, and so
tone down the colored feather splash to avert the heavenly gaze.
Use earthy tones, like gape of crow, and shun the oriole's blaze.
The slow skydive of water birds: for this, kingfisher blue.
In homage to the rising sun, some phoenix feathers too.
Stretch the feathers over wax. Stitch around the frame.'

The sun looked down. And Icarus came.

II   *A daughter sings from the earth*

My mother shoots birds for their feathers,
sometimes crows for their size and their sheen.

She'll crouch by the lake in all weathers
to bring down the right shade of green.

I arrive home from school; it is teatime.
Her warm gun still smokes by the door.

I find her hunched over her pluckings
while my sister sweeps birds off the floor.
As daughters, we both have our duties,
but Icarus, a boy, has got none.

Whatever he does, can't be faulted.
Neighbors say: *A highflyer, that son.*

My dad spends all day in his workshop.
Nearly finished, he whistles and sings.

I can guess what he's making. But I ask this:
Why does Icarus, my brother, need wings?

III   *Ravenous*

How far did you become a bird
when they dressed you in feathers?
When, with beak-bruised fingers,
they drew down onto your shoulders
the great bird mask?

Unhallowed boy, part-raven,
hurled at the heavens, skewered
to the sun's slipstream,
whose was the hunger
that set you off on flight?

As I look along the sky's dark corridor
on starless evenings, your ashy imprint
lurks, spread-eagled against glass.
The crash and burn of bird
become a cruciform of dust.

-- Diana Brodie

The Color of Sound in the City

Gray down on the rooftops,
pock marked and feckle.
The streets, store glass,
white automobiles.
Black heads and blemishes,
acne scabbed and oozing.
The train crossing,
pigeons on the platform,
garbage cans. Splinters,
tears, cracks and holes.
Silence is afterbirth.
Downed wires, downed trees,
a bird's nest and three spilled eggs.
Someone left breathing.

-- Michael H. Brownstein

The Moth

"What did the doctor say?" she asks.
"She says it's a rare bug," he replies,
and just at that moment a scarab moth flies from his mouth,
its wings an iridescent jigsaw of reds and purples and blues.
It flutters for a moment in front of his face.
"Is that it, do you think?" he asks.
"Must be," she replies.

But later, when she opens his shirt and puts her ear to his chest,
she can hear another singing,
pulling at his heartstrings,
making his heart beat fast, light.
And she smiles up into his eyes
but says nothing.

-- Dorothy Burgess

Icarus

He made the joyous leap
and floated
free
momentarily, from worries
flesh-bound.

Brother, now, to all things light
and soaring, he feels
power in shadows
shadows that follow then fade from sight
as he climbs that wide blue highway
narrowing
to a dead end street.

-- Janet Butler

The Visitor

I glimpse a curve of wing
In a fleeting shadow.
See a narrow bare foot, gliding.
Feel the softest touch upon my shoulder
And know that I am not alone.

-- Miki Byrne

The Mind is a Bird's Nest

That winged creature glows cursing
freely at the smothered pillow enduring
death blows.

I eat and eat
the bird that follows the rest
stuffed down
between the fabric until I have nowhere
to lay my head.

A crack in the glass
of the small window.
Rays between
the ammonia filled clouds.

I could choose to
shatter the panes, bloody wings
attempt flight but lie idle the bird
among single feathers
torn from the white sack of surrender.

I could choose sorrow,
to cushion my head under
the shards of reflection
the shades of grey
smoke-stack memories
the down of pigeon fluff,
"Sky's rats," they say.

The sunset after the storm
tells truth more easily than
the spectacles of spectators.

I caught beneath the glass
where it all changes
and I am changed by
cycles
imagined wind tunnels,
dreams of being threaded
through miniscule needle holes;
each smaller than the last until
it cannot pierce
and redeem the pillowcase.

-- Tiffany Chaney

Wax in the Sunshine

Beaks
break the pane of cornea, burning
wings wished upon
by strangers far away,
this
falling star,
hollow bones shattered
on surface tension waters
as I soar past, my
eyes
adding salt to the sea

-- Esteban Colon

Beyond Blinds

Two tone leaves spasm in seizure winds
limbs
rocking, bending
at nigh impossible angles.

Wind,
like a Gemini cat reaches paws into bushes,
bats
airborne plastic bags,
purrs,
crowd surfing a
thousand blades of grass, a
green ocean near night
with waves,
and rising tides.

Birds,
like children dragged through grocery stores are
the first to break the frame,
run
feathers through paint,
smearing
small sections of tapestry
bravely
paving the way for
the occasional sedan, or
minivan who
sits pregnant at the bottom edge, till
silent screams ignite, as she opens
reveals
children trapped inside, exploding out the waters of a river
squeezing
through a quarter sized hole in the damn
while

a full grown woman
emerges more slowly from the front,
mouth a third hand, kicks
the door shut, nucleus
for her
well-trained electron children, swirling
cloud
lapping round her till
the edges of brick, house
like a mountain on the horizon
obscures her from vision,
makes her
cease
to exist.

Sound politely asks glass patio doors for admission
stays
still as sun-bleached chains
whispering
at the edges
through beaks.

-- Esteban Colon

The Bird

we
miss the point entirely.

deaf and proud,
erecting walls like excited phalluses
watching
flickering lights like the birth of new babies,
till

***

we
shake our heads,
mourn
the poor stupid beast,
assuming him less a revolutionary
than
an idiot blind to glass

***

we
miss the point entirely,
fail
to see his limp body
a
sacrifice
to place one
tiny
crack
in our glowing spire.

-- Esteban Colon

My Homing Pigeon Heart

My homing pigeon heart: eternally it wings me
On a long journey back through time
We follow the north star to the lake
Of Neptune's song and mermaid hair
And land beside that ramshackle cottage
With a carport on the side
And the porch with the swing
Where I fell in love
The pigeon heart comes to roost
Atop the broken chimney
It tucks its wings close to its sides
And coos and doves
While I wander through the ghosts
And cobwebs of the carport
To open the back door and walk across
The kitchen's black and white tiles
I see the washing machine that sits by the stove
I hear it churning and wringing
The fabrics of time
There is a parakeet by the window; he whistles in the sun
And because it is a hopeful spring
My father is planting a garden
And my mother is so young
Her eyes sparkle and snap
My brother is playing ball
In the empty lot by the carport
And my sister digs insider her box of paper dolls
She sees that again our bunny has chewed
The dolls' skirts and arms
Then I wander outside, and hear the lake
Of Neptune's song and mermaid hair
I say to the pigeon sitting atop the chimney,
"We must go now for I have lifetimes
Of tragedies and triumphs to live."

But my pigeon heart says, "Why go?"
Always we come back
For don't you remember
It was a spring of hope?
You fell in love on the porch swing
Your father planted a garden
And your mother was so young
Her eyes sparkled and snapped

-- Susan Dale

Of Time

Of time on winged flight
And of the river running beside us
The shadows of our days
Following the sun until it drops off
Into the night skies of infinity
And of the rituals of sand falling
And rippling across indolent deserts
As seen from the window of a train
Entering a tunnel, long and black
To come out into bright sunshine
Leaving behind
In the hollow darkness
A song of the soul
With its melody lingering
Until drowned out by the steel track clamor
Of rolling wheels rounding a bend
Of houses with open doors and window eyes
And the gray ghosts of yesterday
Draped across the rooftops
Of fields flooded with sunlight
Fractured into a million diamond glints
Reflected back by the waters of the river
Yet running along beside us
And beyond us to empty into
The vast and deep oceans of our beginnings

-- Susan Dale

Losing Feathers

I fall back
naked and spread
white wings fold back like hotel sheets
peach velour blanket on skin
bedside lamp shines on Pizza menu
and corkscrew borrowed from the front desk
secrets wet the borrowed bed
voices in my ear
I turn neck into shoulder
but I know right from wrong
that it's silly to sleep with someone
I can never love
especially when each time
I trip and fall
on his hardness
impale myself blissfully
someone else is feeling the shaft
a blade in the back
tossing sleepless from nightmares of truth
I may comfort him
think him dumb
but he is sharp enough to sniff out my lies.
There is nothing virgin about my wings
they are tainted and tattered
as a gutter pigeon's
I peck and I peck
at the last bit of flesh
bewildered by the strength of my own desire.
It's burn every time
I return
as much as I would like not
to hold the weight of his heart
it's gigantic throbbing pulp
I am flattened by it

can only snake out an arm
from beneath
text an SOS
plan another meeting of bodies
even knowing
blood will shed.

                 -- Cassandra Dallett

Potential

Today is alone with itself in the kitchen.
Any winged thing should be able to fly
to find a safer arrangement, one in which
the hollow feeling is less. Touching
pots and pans, something dropped. Steam
from trembling lids. Some plucked thing turning white.
Booth after empty booth, chairs turned up on tables
like legs of upturned bugs, dead of something
other than the hard sole of a loafer. What fare?
What the bean is there to do? Inexhaustibly inefficient
he asked for aubergine on his artichoke sandwich – more
organs, he said, if you please. A couple at the register
haggling the check. He climbed to the roof, another booth
left empty. Subsequent rungs ring of numb subsequence.
Man, he decided, drinking in the foul city view,
it sure is lonely up here. He shut his eyes,
scents and sounds insisting dreams are real. There is pleasure
is knowing that they will come and there is something left to do.

-- Jim Davis

Fruitfly

As I drank from ancient fountains,
stood before basilicas in wonder,
breathed in the chaos of sprawling frescos

with a certain *belle donne* on my arm,
the fruit flies were having their way
with the trash I forgot to empty

before I left. Those bred in the soft
apples and black bananas of the bin
formed a halo, upon my return, above the rubbish,

at the mouth of sink, the head
of the shower, the calcified pit of the drain.
I used the hem of a blue *Italia* t-shirt

to cover my face as I sprayed
the final inch of Raid from its tall poison can.
Some fell; some lingered.

The noble rhythm of work reassembles
and I fall dutifully into it. Showering dust
from the Monday softball double-header

I notice, enwreathed in orange blossom
scented shampoo, a curious fruit fly tapping dumbly
at the corner of the stall. As I dry and hang

my damp blue towel from the curtain rod,
I see him again, tapping at the mirror. Slowly,
I point at this final fruit fly and wonder

if he was the last egg hatched, searching
for conversation, or the toughest of the bunch,

unwilling to relinquish what spritely times might be

had in the universe of a garden apartment.
Brushing my teeth, bending to spit foam
into the newly clean space of the drain, I am

struck with small pangs of guilt: the mark
he leaves upon the world, undervalued, underwhelmed,
as I press him casually into the glass.

-- Jim Davis

Tread Mark Upon Airborne Cloud

wings, knife edged, cut through rolling cloud, fixed gear squadrons ascend

warbirds that plague me, tire treads leaving tracks apparent on the fluff

> cloudbanks are not for the financially sound in the high places they reach

> through broken windows where they grasp and then gasp, taking nothing in

but an airship cavalcade, bag slung gondolas, fly at safe altitude, above oceans

large silver fish leaping in unison, keeping to the tradition of all swimming bodies

> they move in one direction at a time, avoiding head on collision with things

> unimportant like the defective wings of Icarus piled haphazardly by the exit

my pedal powered whirlybird growing obsolete by the minute standing solitary

in a muddy lane, a broken wheel, menaced only by a passing carriage of time

> rocketing skyward now, catapulted by ingenuous methods of mankind

only to float back, gravity powered mortal flesh in wind arresting sails

to be the lucky one that catches the rainbow, riding its rain slick spectrum down

never to find what lies at the end

-- R.C. Davis

Metamorphosis
with apologies to Franz Kafka

In the morning, Seymour, the pachyderm
awoke to find in his own *Metamorphosis*
that he had grown feathers and tiny wings,
an aquiline beak and three-toed claws in place of bulbous feet;
and so astonished was he and so ashamed
that he locked himself inside his room, vowing never to leave,
to make certain that no one else could see
what had become of him or hear him cluck
instead of rumble and roar; and there he stayed with little to eat
and little else to do than loll in the mud all day
while pondering his fate as his weight once great
became less and less and his body more sleek
and aerodynamically appropriate for flight
until, at last, after several attempts at suicide
by rope, gas, and bird seed laced with arsenic
it occurred to him that he could fly away
become a warbler or a jay or the parakeet
he longed to be in a tropical paradise by the sea;
and so he stood on his window sill, clucked "*bon voyage,
cruel world of my miserable past*"
and leaped into the air, too late to realize that the bird
he had become was a chicken (not even a duck) unable to fly –
farewell, Seymour, goodbye, kerplunk!

-- Neil Ellman

Flight
a haiku series

back on solid land, the
writer balks, tries to shake off
her talent, but can't.

it clings to her skin
like sticky tape, like karma
it won't release her.

better a lawyer
than this! she cries, when the muse
refuses to show.

she longs for wings, white
feathers, to hold hope aloft.
but nothing happens.

no inspiration
no *dues ex machina* to
catch her when she falls.

she's been here before,
the panic after take off
till words tumble out.

outside, there's laughter,
seagulls, then the cocktail hour.
inside, the blank page.

who told her she could
be an artist, anyway?
who said she could fly?

then she remembered.
I knew it, the writer said,
clearly. it was I.

-- Alexis Rhone Fancher

Winds Calm and Variable

Sheltered in the lee of the island you steer the boat out into the westerly and look towards the horizon seeing nothing but stampeding horses within the waves, white foam and green seas. You take a chance today. You have to go out and catch the fish to make a living, to bring home the bacon, to feed the family, to buy new stuff. You've been harbour bound three days to this gale and storm listening to the forecast calling for variable winds easing to calm waters. The wild horses on the horizon tell you different and you point the bow out past the rock piles and into the teeth of the summer storm.

The tiny seventy foot boat, with all hands aboard, steams out past the sea lions basking in the sun. They raise their heads and thick necks to watch the commotion as the bow rises and dips in the tide slop. Who is it crazy enough to go out there they think, and nestle back into the warmth and stink of the pride. The boat, the *Rubicon*, punches on. She takes on water over the anchor winch, spray coating the wheelhouse windows with a layer of salt. You make your way for a good two hours towards the grounds. The wild horses now suddenly upon you turn to green curling seas building high above the smokestack and into the rigging. The crew hangs on to the galley table, making things orderly and just right.

Your chart and sounder say you are almost there. You give the boys a ten minute warning. They step out through the galley door and onto the deck and they hang on. One hand for themselves, they know, and one hand for the boat. The deck heaves and the green, cold seas run in and out of the scuppers. You yell into the noise with spittle running along your face. You yell to be careful and you yell to set the gear, to drop the doors and let the yards and yards of net out past the stern. The *Rubicon* pulls with engines screaming and smoke billowing, the gear bumping along the bottom, destroying coral and pillars of weeds as the net scoops up cod and sole. Below is death and destruction and above is chaos and foam.

You tow for a solid hour, watching the sounder for net tearing crags and stumps. You look skyward and watch the albatross living its life, wings barely kissing the ocean. The hooked beak liver birds fluttering about you wait for a chance to peck at the by-catch thrown over the side. You look at the wonder, all familiar and seen before, and you start hauling back, first the wire warps and next the doors. The mouth of the sock-like net enters the stern chute. You look astern and the cod end pops up and bobs like driftwood in the following sea. The seagulls attack the end, hoping for a bite before it disappears. You open the starboard wheelhouse door and enter the storm and your breath is swept away. You try to yell but the words are thrown into the water. The boys split the net and open the end with a single pull to the knot.

The load of fish spreads out on deck like an avalanche and you see dollars for you and the boys. Somewhere down below you hear the victory whoops and hollers and you manage to add your voice. "Hurry up", you shout, "before we're pushed a mile to the lee". The *Rubicon* heaves and jumps in the gale, now almost a storm force. You try to set one more time before turning away and into cove, but the monster Cats in the engine room can't turn the bow into the monster storm. You turn and go with it and the net comes up clean and empty and you spool it back onto the drum.

You've turned away now, away from the storm, the wind. With your tail ever so slightly tucked away, you bow to the weather, thankful that you'll be out there to fight another day.

-- Mike Florian

Sex in Midair

Catkins from the oak tree
   lie scattered on my deck, blown
into piles – all that flaccid
      sex, spent

after dispensing pollen into the air,
   on cars, tickling noses, just to impregnate
tiny, female flowers which
      gestate the fabled acorn.

Too bad oaks don't have as much fun
   as male doves, necks puffed up,
chasing their mates across my patio,
      or mockingbirds in the yard

whose aerial courtship rivals the balletics
   of the Navy's Blue Angels.
One of these days there will be
      a female Blue Angels pilot,

   and the Navy might get suspicious
when planes disappear
      behind clouds.

          -- Patricia L. Goodman

Cold Hope

    He glides
across the pond,
       great grey wings set,
eyes on the bare spot
       on the bank,
a perfect place to land.

    The air is still, so cold
starlings in the old walnut
       huddle, silent
against the heavy sky.

    The heron lands,
lifts his lanky legs
       as he walks to the frozen edge.
He's hungry, but there will be
       no meal here.
The ice is three inches thick,

       yet he keeps walking,
one smooth step, another,
       out onto the ice,
ducks slow motion
       around tawny rushes
frozen where they grew,
       until he vanishes from sight.

    I think about the biting cold,
his empty belly,
       how he must know
there's open water at the inlet,

just a few more
silent steps away.

-- Patricia L. Goodman

Flipping Grief the Bird

Two goldfinches sit at breakfast, mirror
        images on my window feeder.
Doves scout for dropped seed,
        a downy woodpecker hangs
    upside down from the suet – sometimes
      the only friends I see

all day. Surprise flurries
        alight in the birdbath. Three deer
dash across the backyard, spooked
        by a man in a dark parka,
    just as I want to run from grief.

But look, now morning sun explodes
        through the woods, long shadows
    of trees reach out, touch
        each other. The day
awakens, new discoveries
        nestled beneath its wings.

                -- Patricia L. Goodman

Invocation

Give me wings
and I will soar above the earth
as unrestrained as eagles;
like peregrines, zip across the sky
with lightning speed,
hang like gulls
on seaweed scented breeze,
zigzag snipe style
above an island marsh
with feathers drumming
in the evening air;
or ride Spring skies as ravens do,
turn upside down, free fall
then right myself again.

If in need of company
I'll skim, with shearwaters,
the troughs and crests of ocean waves;
with swifts I'll scream and split the skies.
Or on the seashore, join a dunlin flock
to rise, wheel, curve and swing
in perfect unison.
And at days end I'll sail,
       soft, slow,
               on silent wings,
to haunt at dusk,
       the twilight fields
             with owls.

                     -- *Mavis Gulliver*

Eucalyptus

The trees frightened me at sundown
when they turned to a black iron ship
towering over the flat ocean of purple
vines. A few white tall trunks stood out

from the grove's edge and sometimes
something bright flickered at a high
turret, a red-tailed hawk's flashing
outstretched underwings. And once

a year a thousand turkey vultures circled
a mile above the woods that were a stop
on their migration route, though where
did vultures migrate, and why? Home

for crows and hawks, especially owls
at evening the blue gums echoed
with the massed voices of sparrows
robins, in springtime greedy starlings

returned from stripping an orchard
of green plums. At dusk in winter
across the bare vineyards great flocks
of blackbirds swerved like snapped sheets

their leaders making for the forest
like some giant's weird garden, 20 acres
planted 60 years ago perfectly in rows
for furniture and lumber after the World

War I timber scare. I imagined dim high-
ceilinged rooms smelling of eucalyptus
cough drops, strange big-armed sofas
and chairs, vast indigo tables, malleable

sticky to the touch. The stand went uncut,
the grain twisted, unsuited for building,
and grew 200 feet, shading whole sections
of grapes that starved for lack of light

wilted from the oil leached from blown
gum leaves. A man named Flowers
leased the grove and turned turkeys loose
inside. Morning and evening you heard

their roar, the closer you got the louder
they gabbled until at the chicken-wire
you saw ghostly white birds moving
through the dark. Near Thanksgiving

the noise diminished and by Christmas
it ceased. Flowers had a female cocker
always in heat that drew barking packs. Firing
a shotgun in December Flowers hit six

of the neighbors' dogs. February
my uncle pruned the Santa Rosa plums
and heard yelping, got down from his ladder
climbed the fence to rescue my fox terrier

trapped in a snare. Mike was too small to kill
a 30-pound turkey. A week later he rushed into
the yard, a note tied to his collar: "Go feather your
nest!" We never knew who wrote it or why.

-- Nels Hanson

Full Light

Light of false dawn illumines only the sky,
terrestrial objects are not identifiable, no
shadows are cast.
Light of true dawn is of a different sort,
horizon lines are drawn by contrast,
intervening objects are backlit, seen
only in dark relief, colorless, without
detail, but named.
Light of full dawn; sparrows congregating,
vigorously breaking fast at the backyard feeder.
A red-tailed shadow sends them scrambling,
seeking safety and solace deep within the cypress
bushes and bougainvillea.
No sound was necessary to send the vagrant flock
fleeing in unison, a better maneuver in formation
than practice could create, only the dark shadow of
violence in full daylight looming ever larger,
every moment.

-- Richard D. Hartwell

A Dream of Flight

From early on
I dreamt of flight.
By day I was a puny schoolboy,
by night a man of steel,
cape billowing in full sail,
ears ringing with the wind
as I soared over
toy cars and houses and stores.
From far below
my tiny mother waved at me
and I waved back.

In my super tee,
emblazoned with a bold red "S"
against a field of gold,
I could outrace the fastest train,
overleap the tallest building,
corral the masterminds of crime
as if they were stray mongrels
destined for the pound.

At least by night.

My cousin Lee,
who seldom ran on
all four cyclinders,
determined he would fly by day,
and so he pulled his dyed red undies
over blue pajamas
and climbed up to the roof.
"Don't do it Lee," I cried
but he had already jumped.

We found him face down
in the sandbox
with a broken collar bone
and two bruised arms,
telling anyone who'd listen
that before the ground rose up
to meet him like a bully's fist,
he had tasted for
one brief moment
the miracle of flight.

-- Art Heifetz

When Angels Fly Too Close

Every time I think—
There—I've emptied
Myself for now
Said all the prayers
I know for you
Wept out every tear

Another indignity
Scurries forth
To further incense
Me, thwart
Any pretense
At ambivalence
Or dazed sanity

No matter - I welcome
Back the holy
Tenderness that flies
like a wounded cygnet:
Wings unable to flap
Lungs unready to breathe
It plummets, gives into
Fear and sinks beneath
the water ...

Maybe if I think of you
metaphorically,
in abstracts
the pain will grow
more bearable
I don't believe it,
Not really
but I need
to try

to do something
even just
a little
different

        -- S.E. Ingraham

Anticipating Rionero and the Swallows

Far above the third rock, I doze on and off
Falling in and out of dreams of Italia
Picturing the tiny village where I will
Eventually lay my head, later tonight
I gaze out what passes for a window
On this soaring silver bird and swear
At times, there are swallows diving
Around the plane - swooping close
The way they tend to and with their
Sideways glances, looking in at me
Then swooping away again ...
I know, intellectually, the birds cannot
Be there - at thirty-thousand feet
Any bird would surely freeze to death

Still, I have this lingering impression
Of these winged wonders showing
Themselves time and again, urging me
On - reminding me that I am returning
To a place I have come to love
Perhaps like the swallows of Capistrano
These and me, will be ones that return
Yearly to Rionero in Vulture - I would
Be okay with that - more than okay

-- S.E. Ingraham

Humbling Journeys

great bodies of water seen from the air,
appear like art canvas
brush-stroked or pallet-knifed
cobalt, prussian blue, slate,
pale viridian - to name a few
flying, I feel insignificant
at times like these – hours
of passing nothing but water

the only things seeming as endless
viewed from the air,
are mountain ranges
row on row of snow- covered
peaks, that from 30,000 plus feet
appear somewhat the same height
could as easily be waves as peaks
it is illusory but equally humbling

at times the unendingness
of it all has the propensity
to make me feel diminished
and I find I can't help but think
about dear brave Amelia Earhart
flying off into the great
unknown – radioing
to land that she and her
co-pilot were lost but
not that worried –

and then, they were
never seen
nor heard from, again

-- S.E. Ingraham

The Feathered Poet

Late twilight in the backyard
A crow swoops low as I rake up
The last pile of leaves
Bird flocks wing south
And yet on the telephone wire
Is one who did not
Follow his kind
One who ignored
His better instincts
And turned his back
On mere survival
Strange bird of sadness
Why do you stay to sing
When only I who
Do not understand your words
Am left to hear you?

-- Ken L. Jones

Will

I dreamed you
before
I knew you –

        the sloped back
        of your feathery
        crown,

        the downy nape
        above
        your braided spine,

        the slippery wings
        beneath
        your delicate shoulders –

already
behind you,

already
charmed

by your
effortless
flight.

                -- Lora Keller

What Remains

There's a flutter, a
staccato hum, in
my breast.

Nothing solid grows,
I'm sure. No rusty,
spiked germ.

Airy like a silk
moth, beating her new
grey wings,

she thrills to escape
my pillowed cavern;
to drench

her throat in ripe, sweet
nectar; to test the
night sky;

to grant me her coil
of precious thread, to
unwind.

-- Lora Keller

Your Best Bow

My almost-cleavage
peeks from the scoop neck,
the Peter Pan collar,
the snug bodice.

Tiny cerulean daisies dot
the maiden-white cotton
of this, my first
store bought,

procession-perfect dress
for my eighth grade
graduation
from St. Aloysius.

The Cinderella-blue sash
trails down the sides
of the slim skirt
like two extra arms

as I find you
in the kitchen.
A gingham apron
protects your lap.

You rush to me
and lift the ends
from the dingy
linoleum.

You kneel
at my patent leather toes.
My tender ribs
brace your cheek.

Your arms circle my waist,
your hands behind my back.
You loop and loop, tie and knot,
where neither of us can see.

You twirl me around
and fluff the tangled ends
into a bow,
fluid and airy.

Then quickly you turn
toward the sink,
already blind
to my soft,
splendid
wings.

-- Lora Keller

Empire of Trees

Ears battered to
silence.
Your mystery voice: icy
wind above the towers of moon.

Drowned sailors
rise
in a circle of liquid
pearl, their tongues, those

carpets of flesh
tasting moans or songs

words bobbing, then submerged
in the black brine.

No day to enter the
world
with a long beard or
a message to sing, no day

to fly into stars, vision-maddened
crow
ascending by wing
beats to the empire of trees.

-- Steve Klepetar

On the Wing

My mother is afraid for me, but my stepfather says, "He's going to be a man soon. If he wants to go, let him."

So I'm on the plane alone. A stewardess with white skin and orange hair keeps leaning around her work station to smile and wink at me.

The man in the middle seat has gas and smells like cow manure. He wears a smudged ring and I wonder if he's someone's father.

Where I'm flying to is flat farmland. Acres of wheat. Tractors and combines. In the winter the snows get so deep that locals drive snowmobiles on the streets instead of cars. I've never been, but I know because my blood father wrote me long letters that I'd find torn up in my parent's trash.

When I tell the stewardess I'll be nine in June, her smile lifts like it's a hard trick she's doing. "I've got a daughter just your age. You're pretty brave to be flying by yourself." I don't agree, but I don't say so either. I just think I'm maybe desperate.

I saw an old film reel of a man walking across the wing of an airplane as it flew in the sky. After a while it got boring, but then the clip changed and he was pedaling a unicycle while gigantic gusts threatened to toss him off. My stepfather called the man a jackass and said, "That's the dumbest thing I've ever seen."

The stewardess brings me a ginger ale. The bubbles won't stop popping over the rim of the plastic glass. "What are you going to do in North Dakota?"

I tell her my real father lives there. I tell her I've not seen him in person that I can remember. I don't tell her that my stepfather hates me and I hate him back. I tell her lots of things, except how I'm on this bird and I'm never returning.

I've lied to my mother about this trip. She thinks my father will be waiting for me at the airport when we land. She thinks he helped plan everything and that I'll only be gone a week. Lying's not as easy as people think.

The man beside me pulls out his laptop. He holds it close to his chest, flat over his huge belly. There are all kinds of naked women on the screen. How he thinks I can't see them is a wonder, or maybe he doesn't care.

After a while he gets up to use the restroom, so I take his cup of coffee and pour half of it over his laptop's keyboard, then set the cup back. If he asks, I'll say it was the turbulence.

When I look out my window, it's a wall of white and the clouds are threatening to suck up the wing. I imagine that I'm out there, riding a unicycle and that people are watching, that they care. I pretend they're cheering and shouting my name and this makes me the happiest I've been, maybe since forever.

-- Len Kuntz

Flute Carved from the Wing Bone of a Red Crowned Crane

wing-born   born to/of flight   inheriting wing

loft bone . . →

swirling through swaths of cumulous gong

shedding terrestrial surfeit marrow pilings

sledding through mnemonic collections

a whir construction,

                      séanced to lift

to robe the tribe aloft

                          [the flute is a wind instrument

traveling with :: migrating

     {Olatunji/the African drum migrates

      Sabicas/the Spanish guitar migrates

      Casals/the Italian cello migrates

        Dolphy's flute in "Left Alone" migrates

wind is breath, is chicory & due diligence, is sough & surreption, circ-u-la-tion & suspense, is Everywhere, & absence's apologia flute: built to fly like the crane

the flock migrating South hear it

    → scaling kinship glissades hurling from rotational telekinetic watchtowers

hear:

    → rumbling lurch-routed wail-plaints from the fallen,

    the left behind

hear:

    → the benumbing rush to altitudinous sagacity spike,

a last ditch heave discing coloratura songster stars thick with anthem,

braiding tunefuls of

scorch-lament

        to

restore

        umbilical

breach

Note: Playable tonal flutes dated around 7,000 BCE have been unearthed at Jiahu, the site of a "Neolithic Yellow River settlement based in the central plains of ancient China. The flutes were made from Red-crowned Crane wing bones."

    -- Heller Levinson

Mongolian Eagle's Ascent

In Mongolia, a group of Kazakhs hunt with golden eagles, a tradition more than a thousand years old. Females are employed because they are believed to be more aggressive and, weighing as much as 15 pounds are nearly a third heavier than males. Once trapped, taming her is difficult. Her ankles are bound in leather straps and tied to a wooden block on a rawhide line. Each time she tries to fly away, she flips upside down. She'll stay struggling with this tightrope for up to two days. When she's exhausted, she's tame, and the falconer can teach her to return, bloody knuckled after a hunt.

-- National Geographic

"To soar by cutting --

my talon tips pouring thousands of pounds

of pressure per square inch -- hares, mice --, snake --

this manicured death quash lifts

permits my aerial dives & dips partnered

by ancient scrolls unribboning encrypted simoom *davenings*

the flipping cornerstones of the igneous mute

    -- contra-horizon decibels

      lute clouds

      strum precipitations

tongues elaborate -- prickled into form --

            over the feast

something about the carcass, a table

of dead matter, that fires speech

seals transport that engines

these seven feet of outstretched wing

stabilized with swoop considerations

            privileged lookout

            conspiratorial advantage

bellying glee merchandise over the Hovd river

shoaled in magisterial buoyancy

and now

routed to feed

surviving through speech-preemptive strikes

carouseled by a perpetual hegemony

I

am

tied

netted through the spear of my hunger

raveled in the thorn comfort station

                 -- digestive hackery

tethered to their delectables-table

my vitality cropping up as a tin soldier at a shooting arcade

[*the underbelly of sustenance is erasement*]

'eat to be devoured'

stunned by a specimen exceeding their peremptories

ambitions are reformulated

they have big hopes for me

(expansion plans

soon to hood my vision-feasting with rufter

to dismast my winged alacrity my tipping

hilarities to the Altay mountains alive with oneiric celebrity

apophainesthai

nikkhamitva

ascent is rallying thermals

is feathered incarnadine inception

like the movement of Arlesian

sunflowers

posting madrigals from my primaries

the nine streams of ontic cuneiform

saturate spent misanthropic legacies

distal kingdoms of divisibility shatter

in original emergence

words rousing at the world's ignition

loading the wings with significance

                -- molt perspecuities

they taste my fatigue

croon in upon my weariness

my culpable biology

Coyote Becomes -- *OTHER* -- Than The Willed

and with hot verbs calligraphying my wing

I scrum the playing cards of Falconiform ancestry

rostering strength to scrumble hurls of negation

a resistance so profound

that

in that moment I bolt upright

that they will count as energy Spent

my flapping will mount so severe

I will lunge into a nano-second of flight

delivering to them

a carcass"

while for myself

I reserve

a scrupulously articulated

soar"

                       -- Heller Levinson

Morgan's Birds

In the almost tallest tree, Morgan's birds wait.

sky near full blue but for clouds come from all the way west
tangled up with sea shape breezes tasting salty even here.

yellow wasps angry buzzing in but rarely back out the kitchen windows
maybe unable to remember it's only august and wild
apples by the dozen still lay strewn along the back garden.
rugosa roses stretch up the stone of this house
where through the last while of the day
sun hits strongest.
sometimes my own fingers search out along those warm textures as if
attempting to discover something they need to know until
I must say thank you right out loud with out even figuring out who to.
in the almost tallest tree, Morgan's birds wait.
they have time to be patient, preening, cackling, shifting branches
occasionally engaged in soft arguments,
remind me of some vague song until
like a shipwreck in the sky they rise.

-- pd lyons

Intelligent Design

Yesterday I learned of centrioles, tiny tubes,
within our cells that hold
together parts of our DNA. No one can quantify
what exists inside those tubes
but there must be something –
very little of our bodies are wasted
space. We are chock-full of practicalities.
Scientists think maybe
these tubes hold consciousness.
If this is true, cells release it
when we die. Like dandelion fuzz, floats
up out of cells, bodies, flies
away from us, into space –
back where it came from, star stuff.
I find comfort in the thought
that upon those same wings goes
the pain of trauma during abuse. Our cells
expel the burden, beyond
the boundaries of known physics, give
the gift of temporary flight.

-- Jacqueline Markowski

Kingfisher

Blue, so intense it burns the eyes.
A spear of laser light
plunging on the unsuspecting sprat,
shattering the mirror pool
into a million kaleidoscopic pieces.
Slowly they spin in ever circling patterns
until at last the wheeling surface silvers over,
settling to its former glassy self.
The while, the glistening bird
sits on a branch,
so beautiful you catch your breath,
so cruel you lose your life.

-- Joe Massingham

The Hawk

The hawk hangs on a slow moving cloud,
looking down, searching for breakfast.
A mouse, scuttling along the path
he's worn through the wheat,
doesn't see the glinting eye or
downward dive, nor,
because the hawk drops
faster than the speed of sound,
does he hear death coming.
Snack finished, blood licked
from his beak, the hawk rides
a thermal escalator
until he rests on cloud nine again.

-- Joe Massingham

Look Homeward, Thomas

Can you immortalize an angel,
shadowed cement wings and
right hand dripping dust,

brought by the writer's father
from under the Italian cypresses of home
to stand here blessing passers-by

in a North Carolina graveyard?
No, Wolfe immortalized only his
own words, and the angel merely watched,

as, raising a dusty hand, he watches still.

-- Janet McCann

Wildflowers

Bobbing in open fields.
Two fabulous daffodils sprout
from your eyes. Falling dizzy in
love as o so lackadaisical
breeze tugs at shirt sleeves.
Again we are flushed in
warm love caress. Solar
energy orbiting billions of
grass blades. Hum hum
hummingbirds hurry hurry
pass us tripping giddy
in love.

-- Joan McNerney

Another Message from a Harpy Eagle

Ten years ago I first encountered him, isolated,
on a manmade perch without female, shackled
out of place and time in the San Diego Zoo.

Today we meet again, again by chance, again
by subtle fate. This time, for this rare second coming,
I am the stranger in this strange green place on Earth.

The barbed wire and iron bars of his chain-links captivity
have dissolved into strangling liana vines, sky-scraping leaves
of cecropia trees, blistering bush, and bristling bromeliads.

Urban bustle of California is supplanted
by the monkey rustle of the Rio Negro in Brazil's flooded
Igapó forest. He flies; I enter his habitat, on *his* terms.

Aboard an Amazon canoe, slowly floating, adrift,
I round a bend, glimpse him lift from understory snag
and shriek into full view from the tangled darkness

into the river of sifted light – and back again.
He escapes my invading gaze. He stalks more natural prey.
Rara avis, hooded predator masked, is master of this jungle.

He is not the same one I once met. But he *is*.
Reason cannot tell me this is not the same bird,
his feathered message the same a decade later.

Though his mate awaits, he pauses on a limb bridging
the waters to speak of taloned mercy
upon me, my kind; *H. harpyja*, liberated, keens.

                                        -- Karla Linn Merrifield

...he Amazon Avian Checklist Station

...caracara? *No.*
...ed chacalaca? *Not yet.*
...macaw? *Yes.*
A ruckus stirs. *Where?*
Insistent, *Homo sapiens* subspecies *birdus nerdus*
squawks, *I most certainly did. Left bank.*
Rio Yanayacu. In a ficus tree.
Many feathers ruffle.
Then *H.s. competitus* boasts,
My mottled owl is omitted on this list.
Indignant *H.s.* of the jealous race attacks,
You saw one? When? Got a photo to prove it?
Forgotten are pootoo, ani, jacamar,
toucan, and cotinga. No peep about parakeets.
The troupe of apex primates devolves into squabbles,
more squirrel monkeys than human beings.

-- Karla Linn Merrifield

Feathered Friend Fibonacci

stork
kite
egret
anhinga
of Everglades, of
Amazon, birds of my new worlds

-- Karla Linn Merrifield

Morning Song

a bird squawks out of my heart
a dinosaur screeches out of my chest
as I hop in the mirror

squawk squawk
screech screech
go the beings inside

my eyes seeing primordial swamps
my arms bouncing off branches

my babies in a nest
under the eave
on the arid plains
of Patagonia

the genes
the plane of thought

the listening

the biting of my arm

                     -- Bradley Morewood

3112 Archipelago Lane

four red dinosaurs visit me in a drought
as I shower my jasmine with a hose:
the parents place their fledglings near the spray

the young birds flap and snuggle in their feathers
cleaner and cooler
as I direct more water toward them

in the brains and cells of these cardinals is a memory:
eons ago their evolutionary siblings
perished on a shattered Earth

and now on the margin
of the vast radiation of living things
they commune with a fellow survivor

-- Bradley Morewood

Winged

Feel the rising air
stiff against your feathers,
as you drop into earthly space,
adapted muscles pull up, thrust down,
three dimensional volumes to soar in,
to bank into and cavort with,
to scope prey from,
then plummet towards and seize upon,
conferring death for ready food,
the eternal exchange for existence.

Adrift on changing winds,
changing landscapes,
use the loft and take rest,
if migratory, you must,
searching for beacons and marsh.
Every entity designed for flight,
hollow bones, hollow feathers,
but warm blood,
and a heart that soars
in the wind.

-- Heidi Morrell

Bird Lessons

At my grandma's house in Eaton
there were two bird feeders
outside her kitchen window.
She also had a wren house,
and a mansion for Martins.

She was the first person
in my life that paid attention
to birds, fed them, and gave
them shelter.

She bought me my first bird
book to help me identify,
the birds that would flock
to her feeders.

Grandma was pleased when
I recognized a black-capped
chickadee or a tufted titmouse,
harder to spot than common
sparrows or striking cardinals.

She called starlings, "dirty birds" –
to scare them off
she made grandpa hang pie
tins in front yard trees
to spin and startle.

Grandma didn't care
for the "mean" blue jays –
who chased her favored
birds away.

Secretly, I loved
those big blue bullies,
and I knew their "caws"
above all others.

                 -- Lylanne Musselman

Memory

One day when I was five
my feet grew light,
and barely treading air,
I left the earth.

The neighbor's naturtiums
turning their mouths, their
nonexistent eyes to watch me,
level almost with the wires,
pairs of knotted hightops
the ginko's butterfly
leaves, white shreds of cloud . . .

    Just then

I looked down at the distant street,
where lawns burned green;
tiny people waved, tempted
me to stop slow drifting
and return to pitiless time.

                -- Robbi Nester

Newcomers

In the Queen Palm's swaying crown
of heavy on the pine boughs
I always hear before I see them,
the wild green parrots from elsewhere.
Only an odd flash of bright
wings, like a sunset trick of light.
No ordinary flock, but only remnants,
my mother's mismatched teacups.
They gawk in groups, like tourists,
nothing in common but being
out of place. Somehow,
they find familiar trees:
the bulbous silk tree, clad
in clouds of silver fluff,
the calm magnolia, with its
lacquered leaves, those immigrants
from everywhere, and eat
the tender fruits and seeds.
I hear the raucous calls and know
that life will always thrive:
moss between the sidewalk cracks,
or tree of heaven growing spinkly
through the sewer grate.

-- Robbi Nester

The Sibyl to Her Fowl

As usual, the marketplace is full-
gawking rubes with mysteries to solve.
Cursing and praying, they offer up their gold.
I in turn fling up the golden grain
luring your wayward flocks out of the trees.
This toss will tell me what I know.

The crowd surveys the twisting
guts of sheep, strewn seeds, even your
broken flight, but sees no pattern there.
My eyes are trained – they see the frozen stars
spell out the night, unraveling ballets of answer.

Our understanding differs about eggs,
the earth, but on this matter, we are one.
I split this seasoned riddle on the tongue.

-- Robbi Nester

Peregrine

Your yearning is a peregrine
seeking, lost, and sought
From within your heart
exquisite longing raises
lithe wings into terrains of
emptiness, of divine rights
melting into blood and
passions, melting into holy
mischiefs within the fierce
wicked funhouse of poetry

-- ayaz daryl nielson

Old Crow and I

conifer
split by lightning
old crows bicker

hot breeze
through the skylight.
   raucous crow

in the oak above
this flat tire
   crow being crow

oh snitty crow,
   was my brief presence
      really so troublesome?

tell me where you live,
   old crow, so I can poop
      on <u>your</u> front porch

crow above
   the new Zen garden
      drops his blessings

new home
same old
crow sounds

old crow and I
   cawing, laughing as we
      meet once again

                        -- ayaz daryl nielson

Wings of Immortality

It was the happiest of beasts
born of the blood of Medusa,
and of the froth of the sea.

Are we not born of our own volition?

This winged horse enjoys liberty.
It gallops above the stratosphere and ionosphere
and whooshes through air like a molecule of wind.
Tireless messenger, it condescends
to swoop to earth and quench his thirst
at its coolest sources and prance about
on the most green of grasses.

Why is her grass greener?
Why are her waters so irresistible?

Poets worship this luminous creature
whose gracious flight evokes purest inspiration.

Why do we need inspiration?
Shouldn't a Muse be natural?

Once upon a time, with a single stroke of
his hoof, Pegasus made a spring on Hélikon,
the mountain of the Muses.
Hippocrène she was named
and a stupendous source she became.
Anyone who drank its water was blessed with
the marvelous grant of poetry.

So is that what it's all about?
We seek to create our personal source?
So how come we drink so much from the others?

Where do we look for immortality?
Are we destined to learn forever how to fly?

-- Alex Nodopaka

Two Dogs Chained

Wolf eyes, fox eyes,
I see you glare at the sun
then wag your tail,
uncertain how to begin your escape.

Let me tell you the ways I've found;
I've jumped the fence more than once myself.

Lay on your belly and wriggle under
the wall in the furthest corner of your brain.

Think like water,
run down the hill in a puddle.

Make yourself small,
slip past where the steel wires meet.

Or think like air, and simply rise up,
over the houses and treetops,
with your eyes fixed on a distant cloud.

Don't spend your life at the end of a leash.
Fly to the hills. Bay at the moon.

Leave them wondering how you did it.

-- Selena Parrish

White Vessel with Inverted Triangle
(After White Vessel With Inverted Triangle, Ceramic, Gordon Baldwin, 1989)

God's man bird –
Stricken in the scrubbed light.
Starved of the air
   that played with his feathers
      like the jibes of children.
White on white in snow bleach.

Hug your smashed wings
and listen through the ice
To the earth song
To a whale's mewl
To the snowblind rush of wind
To Powderface;
the councilor of fallen whispers.
To the dying jabber w*rds
as the last sn*wflake melts upon your tongue.

                     -- Winston H. Plowes

Légende

The night of the being, when thunder is
a sounding board for the moonglade that seeps

into unseen flaws. A hundred unsaid words
in lightning bolts that rip reflections, distortions

a fracas that the rain paints on window glass,
in neon drops that glide downwards into emptiness

of a widening dark. Nothing fits. I dare dream.
Hush; listen to the rain riding the winged

birds of shadows, their white throats that open
and close in unison; their song, their each note

each chord, each fragment of their crescendo
that echoes in myriad harmonious echelons

octaves, arias that my heart chooses
to rise and fall and roll as would a pearl

onto sable colored silk that this night is
and this self is... a swoon of the swayed

in the wide wakening of possibilities. A streak

of thunder ignites the restlessness of my wings

                         -- PratimaBalabhadrapathruni

Nervous Anticipation

I sketch a woman in nude, perched on the railing, the folds of her skin, wrinkles, dimples, contours, navel, the angles of limbs, hair; the bold stare of wide eyes mellowed in colors of dejection, then add houses, chimneys, windows and the bustle of everyday streets, far below.

"Look Honey," I say to him, holding up the sketch. "It is me and my work, vulnerable, bared and pared to our skins, under their microscopes." He waits, reading me like an old book with new nuances.

"How did I measure up? It feels like I have jumped off the cliff, toppled off this railing, steep dived downwards, a thousand leagues from hopes to despair. I am choking; a mutant fish gasping in thin of air." I pause with steeples for brows, a goldfish pout for a mouth. He smiles.

"Will I sprout wings mid air, garner enough strength to fly high?" I swirl, hands raised in a fluid flutter, face hidden by rebellious fly-away curls.

"The smelting process," he says, laconic as ever, planting a kiss on my forehead to heal my lips into a smile, conjuring stars from the shadows in my eyes.

"Go fly, Angel," he says and walks away, leaving behind dissipated haloes of love.

In the background, the wail of an ambulance blends in with the choir of church bells.

-- PratimaBalabhadrapathruni

Prayer

My sights have been lifted
toward a stellar cathedral
in a world without end,
an open door to the soul
of one who searches.

I pluck the soft daggers
from a millennium sky
to shear myself open,
peel away this ashen gray nest
of wounded flesh

& dissolve
within the funnel eye
of absolute light and energy;

surrender my allegiance
to empirical knowledge, my tired
arrogance cloaked in velvet robes
of quiet despair,

to take the blind leap
out of my decaying mortal element
with hands clasped, forming
silver wings

to enter the enigmatic realm
and the light of living waters.

Naked before the arc
of the flaming altar,
I am bathed in the presence
of a steady radiance, touch

of wet silk;
immerse into the echo
of infinite wisdom,

the sound of my own voice.

                -- Ben Rasnic

The Price of Flight

winged beauty frozen in a dream of sunlight
pulling from all directions at once,
     capturing her perfectly & opening
her form
to imagination, the clarity of pixilation,
redemption floating free in a molting blur of feathers
   turned to snow & drifting through the signature of
oxygen—
wispy cirrus-fluff, windblown
       from some distant-star landscape of
her soul;
she glides over sand & rock,
     her descending, dark humanness an
illumination
by virtue of being there
       & the song of her shadow
makes mountains preen iridescent colors & cracks the
desert
      open to the dynamics of
thermal uplift—
the sun & wind blended around a body
   that possesses an allusive mix of ambition &
optimism

   —ascent,
          framed
wholly
  by the beckoning air of the unknown.

immortal daughter of Icarus:
     *angel come down from heaven
yesterday,*

fallen from an endless crescendo of dreams
                         through good-time jazz & molten
2AM blues,
wings expanded to hold whatever still trembles—
still breathes & orbits asteroid-like—
                         19 million miles from
the Son,
closer than any other orbiting folly to a fault,
                         where gravity
follows laws
that have not yet been discovered,
that have not yet been written—
                         a connection of zero, where all
nothingness
or something-ness
comes closer to the all than the hollowness of faith.

       heaven's blue,
wings of feather & wax,
                             the nostalgic
price of flight.
alive,   in the hollow secret of
her bones,
reborn, the repaired redemption of fly far   & fly fast.

          -- henry 7. reneau, jr.

Red
for sabrina macias, on lock-down

a caution shade of combustion all appetite:
Revlon red lipstick that mimics arousal &
pornographic, vermilion fingernails
accentuate a splayed erotic;

red hair kissed by flaming fire,
a sensual awakening, Ann-Margret's purr,
a perfect flint to start a quarrel, or bullet
that portends a war;

fist-tight crimson resurrected & flung
into scorching solar wind,
white phosphorous phoenix, all molten red
& gold immolation.

& frightened russet sparrows
running red-light scared
& brushfire sweep of abandon-ship crows
launch into arsonist auburn sky,

before an obsession with the pyre, terror-blind
terrific as all Creation.   ascending angel ablaze
& dancing as Divine, a red rebellious heart
burning, rising from the stake, to cardinal
conflagration,

to red-shift reincarnation
at the igneous end of panic, scarlet obsession
to vaporization,

to crematoria bone-gray ash, reborn

an unrequited, yet intimate, act of passion.

(**Note:** quoted song fragment by Jimi Hendrix)

-- henry 7. reneau, jr.

An Extraordinary Machine

a dragonfly's erratic hyperbole
and da Vinci imagined helio-copters,
repeatedly traveling a metaphorical tightrope
from the whorls at his fingertips.

sycophantic angels cited divine condescension
from some eternal watchmaker
creating worlds under thumb;
but helio-copters carry Hellfire missiles,
an extraordinary machine

-- henry 7. reneau, jr.

13 Miles to Somewhere

Once left clumps of hair on the pillow.
Convinced myself that this was where it was supposed to grow.
I finally learned that not to be the case.
Conjectured other mysteries worth investigating.
A sign cropped up on a highway 13 miles to somewhere.
Treated it as an omen when I passed Integration,
population someone had crossed out.
Roadside littered by a hodgepodge of scree like hair left on a pillow.
Somewhere over the rise, Integration,
next hillock could be harboring a town for wholeness.
Felt the need, as the miles crept along for integration.
Wind rolled-towel-slapped at my head, met
endless array of clacking teeth, cast-offs chattering in the Boreas.
meaty, fingerless hands like miniature Saguaro cacti grew from the earth,
plinths buried in the sand supported the sky,
cat's eye-marbled apertures peeped from the earth followed me,
miles of intestines wrapped slimily about the landscape like Christmas light strings.
Dis-integrated beings pulverized into the soil where no heaven or hell exists
Only this landscape of randomly sprouting parts.
Integration, asphyxiated cell choked into non-existence,
DNA declares it a *do not admire* zone,
no Frankenstein to re-animate it,
Integration only a sign on the road to nowhere.

-- *Sy Roth*

PMT3 – August 2010

    Up
    there
    a bird of
    steel and iron.
    Water under our
    feet set on a blue mat
like the azure of the sky, soothing, so soft
    in the air liner. Summer
    is leaving us while we
    are entering winter
    all verdigris
    upside
    dow
    n

                        -- Walter Ruhlmann

A Wing Can Cover All Sorts of Things
Title borrowed from Tori Amos's "Sister Janet"

Apparently there is no other way to find shelter than in your arms.

While I idle on the bed mooning over the angels that once came with all their feathers,
I also brood because nothing seems good enough for you and I just wish sometimes
No horizon would seem so appealing as to make you want to fly away.
Granted that once there you will be bored again.

Cowardice is such a plague to deal with
Another defects of mine sewn on the canvas of my formative years
Nth wrongs I can't seem to get rid of.

Could you forgive me if these new angels made of plastic, made of paper,
Outrageously handsome, were to invade our ship?
Voluntarily, lipping, mouthing, tonguing that whitened skin of mine.
Ethereal, I would land in the veils you stretched once to catch me.
Randomly, they would follow me in these nets, hailing at you too on their way back.

Astutely, you would have put on your whitest teeth
Large smile, lard ass,
Lustful little loon

Surely you would slap my face and spit at it too
Overwhelmed by anger and jealousy, not
Resisting your wrath against
The
Stoutness of my desire for other birds of prey.

O,
Forlorn spirit!

The story of my life is one of misunderstanding, anger and rebellion,
Harassment, Tiredness and Spleen – my three very best friends.
I know these thoughts might just melt like snow in Spring, though you should
Never underestimate the passions burning inside, fuels for life,
Generating all spirit that make us all go forward.
Sometimes I think I should just grow wings and reach for the azure sky.

-- Walter Ruhlmann

Hummingbird in the Bookstore

Just browsing, a hummingbird, solo,
on its way south, flits into a bookstore,
examines dictionaries, bestsellers,
puzzles, the latest fiction, darts over
a customer's cap, lights in a hair-do,
investigates earrings, wishing for flowers,
hoping for insects, above all a shrub,
tries cookbooks, greeting cards, maps
are useless, flashes iridescence
as the cash-register ca-chings, panics
near the ceiling, which is not the sky,
like all creatures, yearns for light
and the path made clear.

-- Elizabeth Schultz

Mosquito Obsession

I know where to find her.
I fly to her, then, softly
humming, fluttering,
a sweet briny scent
gives her away to me,
seduces me.
Corpulent and white,
she glows in the dark,
sluggish with sleep.
Cautiously, I approach,
aware of her disdain,
her failure to appreciate
my long legs' delicacy,
my exquisite wings,
my arousal, my life.
Precipitously, she flails
the air, strikes out at me.
And then I come in,
under her arm,
spear her on my kiss,
and suck up her thin,
vermillion blood.
She will remember me.

-- Elizabeth Schultz

Romance

She slathers herself in jasmine oils
and drinks old Bangkok to the lees.
Sun slants decisively through shutters
across her bed. She greets the calendar.
She sojourns with monks and schoolchildren
and sleeps in stone huts on Tibetan plateaus.
She rolls up the carpets and dusts the banister,
saving string and paper clips for a rainy day.
She scoops out papayas on Nairobi verandas,
while discussing AIDS with hospital workers.
The family albums can go to the cousins.
Who cares what happens to the crystal?
She swims with seals in turquoise waters,
later encouraging beachcombing on city streets.
Friends fall. Pelvises crack. She writes notes
of consolation, and moves into retirement.
Still she takes the prow between her legs
and rides into sunsets, sails ablaze.
She cannot lay down her swashbuckling
just yet.

-- Elizabeth Schultz

She Swung Forth to Find the Fall of Night

oft in the field from the day's foes,
under the naked branch, she sat
upon the wooden seat, isolated;
moving in a curved arc, in flight,
without the intent of hitting the air,
she swung forth to find the fall of night;
she changed to endure the
dole of darkness approaching.
that this little girl had heard each
night for fifty years, the din of
revel, high in the heavens, flying,
now came the light to lighten, her
soul to keep forever; the swing
no longer swaying, lifeless.

-- Lance Sheridan
and Barbara Sutton

Smoke from Burning Leaves

brings a knowing-
a certainty there's more

> -- *Carol Smallwood*

A Murder of Crows

On an overcast morning in May,
with light rain and a cool breeze blowing,
I sat alone on a wooden deck,
gazing over a wide salt marsh.
The tide was in its full ebb,
exposing brown banks of mud,
brackets to meandering runnels
cutting their way through the expanses
of greensward formed of *spartina*.
The grass holding stains of mud,
bore witness to the recent spring tide.
A silence lay across the wide marsh,
save for the pitter patter of rain,
suggesting a peace eternal.
Then, out of the void came the cry,
clarion and frenetic, too:
"Caw, caw, caw," again, "caw, caw, caw!"
A mottled brown hawk flew straight and low.
In a fast and frenzied pursuit
came a murder of seven crows.
A raptor was in rapid retreat,
put to rout by seven black bandits.
The hawk flew at medium height,
not skimming the top of the marsh,
not reaching for the heavens
where hawks are wont to soar
in lazy circles far above,
free and lord over prey below.
Now bothered and bullied, it sped
to thick cover in distant pine.
The murder of seven, relentless,
pursued then surrounded the tree.
Safe now, in thick cover of pine,
the osprey perched in dark silence,

while the seven, arranged themselves
in a formation perhaps known
for eons in this avian world.
Each crow took proper position,
as perhaps generations of
its ancestors had done before.
I could but wander if early bands
of warriors thus inspired
had found here tactical lessons
from such bellicose crows.
Each crow, whether in flight,
in chase of this alien hawk,
or in pinning it in its bowery,
seemed to take its assigned place
in this coordinated campaign.
After a time, and one by one
the murder of crows disbanded,
each vocalizing as it left.
The frenetic "caw, caw, caw,"
so penetrating earlier,
was now toned down to a more calm
and conversational "caw, caw."
Donning binoculars, I watched
as one lone crow found a perch
atop a dead tree in the hammock,
some half-mile or so from me.
In seeming patience, it waited.
Presumably, confident that
the skirmish had now been won,
territory made again safe,
the sentry, with muted "caw, caw,"
flew, slowly exiting the scene.
Silence, then a calm conversation
arose between two cardinals.
Being neither crows nor hawks,
these cardinals were but bystanders

to the recently ended affray.
This brings to mind the aphorism,
"Birds of a feather flock together."
And in Norwegian inflection
of said apophthegm most pithy,
giving a meaning less descriptive,
and at once more eroticized,
"Kråke søker make,"
"The crow seeks its mate."
So, we play with the metaphor,
bird and man, and man and bird.
"There are the 'in group,' and the 'out group,'"
so speaks the sociologist.
And, "territoriality,"
quickly adds the biologist.
"It is the 'death instinct!'" cries Freud,
drama added to his earlier
dual-natured formulation,
"aggressive drive" and "self preservation."
Peace shattered and drama played out.
A murder of crows, seven,
and a hawk.

-- Edward W. L. Smith

A Walnut Falls on the Tin Roof of the Mule Stable

The jet breaks sound again.
Black and Gray may be glue, no matter,
at all, but phantoms even to me.
What about you?
When we are old and wrinkled, will the future be caste or class,
idea, memory, song, condition, discussion, voices, problems –

turnips, dirt, collards, bad seed, worries, art,
schools of thoughts, fields, subsoils, roots.
I am writing to him or her whose feelings rage against
Depression,
pushing, retreating, pressing with conviction for aspirations,
some way *toward* Hope.

If I find one foot off balance I sense an inch shall find its way.
What shape are you in?
My scoop's a blade of Somehow.
I hear the jet again: this time it paints Fear.

Your head's buried in talk of detail, insurance, and the like.
The red-bellied sharpens his claws on the pole.
Cricket sniffs for air.
The robin weeps all morning in the meadow.
Still you not yet free: I launch my boat,
pencil in the journey through and over,
around the mockingbird's notes, the purple martins nearby,
jetting into their gourds, while the bluebirds
circle and raise their wings.

Have I not tried hard enough my ride to seek and dock?
Have I not been swimming in the muck long enough?
And, you, I cannot let you go, for you are the dearest to me,
your mind always on the sidelines, not on the ball at all,
and so routine with splendor does not get painted,

though the poem surrounds us, while you ponder the price of meds,
unaware the day or calendar: you stay caught up in *stuff*.

If I could go back beyond the *now* to the girl in Buffalo,
I might not become a victim of our depression,
that gutter stacked with drivel
(big things to you) piling up like jargon in a lecture-hall.

To the Refuse I'll go with my garbage, dump it for recycling.
The world past waits for me to come get it.

Promise to stay clear of raised voices.
Promise to reel clean the expected.
Promise to console scuds entering our soul-zones.
Promise you'll coax the accuser into stilled waiting.
Promise you have heart to sound
reverent tunes over rooftops of communities.
Promise you won't depart me, but keep close
the eternal, the one you have taken on,
hanging family photos on the wall of the middle room of our plankhouse.
The spirit never dies, dissolving and swelling
wisdom like calking between a downspout and a splashboard.
Promise that the aching, pent-up veins

rivering my body
shape one
becoming two, and so one, until Death does its part,
never bringing us closer together,
nevertheless, separate in perception,
seeking solace in the knowledge that you once lived as I.

-- Shelby Stephenson

Also Watched

The ancient oak
beside the coast
unravels to allow
your positioning
like a pure bird
learning its wings.
A blue sea blue
then green and grey rain
awakened like the vigils
of your irises
I also watched.
Sky white cities
fell like a dress
as dark unscrolled,
we held thread
to our shoulders,
star and feathers.

-- John Swain

On the Reed Stalks

Dragged like a globe
from the sea
in your throat,
I rode the storm roads
watching the black sky
crash lightning on the marsh
like an osprey.
Salt on the reed stalks
I gnawed again
for your perfume
in sorrow for dying
as clearing rains wing away
befriended illusions
with all of my tears.
The brackish water
came back upward
through rotten leaves
soft over the pebbles
crushed for luck
by forward moving
into another diamond.

-- John Swain

Air Over Hanoi

Soldiers are filing across the tarmac earlier than scheduled. We just de-planed a load of them from Guam, and now we stews are tearing through the Boeing 707, cleaning up as best we can. Until a few bombs showed up recently, Vietnamese ground service cleaned the planes. In a moment they'll be boarding and our hats aren't on yet.

"Boarding!"

Lana is rummaging through the overhead rack for her hat. "Who put their damn crew kit on my hat! It's crushed!"

We're proud of our hats, wear our wings pinned to them. Stiff blue pillbox hats a la Jackie Kennedy. It's a *stew reg* to wear your hat during boarding and deplaning. Even here in Vietnam. The bulkheads have been yanked out turning passenger planes into troop ships. There's a war going on.

I traded into this trip for the Honolulu layover. I don't hold this line. Stews way more senior than I am hold it; though I can't imagine why. Despite the wet oppressive heat I get a shiver down my spine as the first soldiers climb the plane stairs.

"Don't forget to smile," Margie is saying.

She is twenty-seven and thinks she knows it all. I'm 19 and a half. The youngest you can be to work for this airline. I've been flying less than a year. Mostly Madrid and Lisbon, sometimes London and Paris. In London the hotel towel racks are heated.

I stand beside Margie at what is the first class cabin door under normal circumstances. The first soldier steps in. He looks old around the eyes. We smile and say, "Welcome Aboard."

Some smile back at us, some do not. I begin feeling terrible. I'm sweating from my armpits, across my top lip, scalp, inside my shoes and underwear.

In come the stretchers. Margie keeps smiling; I have to give her that. She smiles through the moaning behind barriers made from bed sheets, where the seats have been removed. Nurses and orderlies are assisting those men. I am told to stay out of their way.

I begin feeling wrecked. I didn't feel wrecked when we came in for landing. I'd looked down and saw the fires burning.

On the first class jumpseat I strap in beside Margie. "How many times have you flown this rotation?" I say.

"A few years."

"A few years!"

She scrutinizes my face. "Someone's gotta do it."

"I suppose."

Finally the plane is starting to cool off. The cockpit door swings open and the flight engineer sticks his head out. "Could one of you sweet things bring me a Coke."

"Sure!" I unbuckle my shoulder harness, jumping up. The Coke can is barely cool; but there's no time to start cracking ice before take-off.

He thanks me with a grin and a wink. "We'll have some fun in Honolulu," he says.

On the jumpseat Margie is having a last cigarette. "The no-smoking sign is lit," I tell her.

"Hon, this is Nam not Dayton ."

I strap back in as the music starts from the sound system: *Up, Up, and Away*. The same music that's always played on take-off and landing. Everywhere. Today it sounds strange, unsettling.

Margie bumps the side of my leg with hers. "It'll be fine."

Suddenly I'm glad to have this senior stew beside me. Even though she carries a little ashtray stolen from out of an arm rest. The other stews laugh behind her back. She catches me looking at the ashtray in her lap.

"We all have our thing," she says. "What about you? Secretly married?" That, too, is strictly against stew regs.

I shake my head. "No. You?"

"Naw. I date a pilot who's married."

I turn toward the cockpit.

"Not them." She smiles. "They're good guys. Always with the jokes, keeping up morale for the men." She takes a few quick puffs. "My guy has a Rome trip this month."

"Why don't you bid Rome ? You have enough seniority."

"His wife is on that trip."
"You mean as a stew?"

"Yep." Then the plane begins to taxi and Margie grinds out the cigarette in her little personal ashtray. "How old are you?"

"Almost twenty."

"Good god."

The plane shudders and lifts, music coming out of the sound system, when the pilot interrupts over the intercom, his voice breaking in static. "Welcome aboard ladies and gentlemen. We are in the air over Hanoi."

A huge roar of laughter fills the cabin. And we lift higher into the sky.

-- Susan Tepper

Calls to Passage*

This evening, late September, light halves the visible.
The vault still rosy and blue and gray, though pierced
through by a quivering point of star, the sidewalk
so dark that streetlights wind leaves already act out
their shadow play.
And this small mass on lawn? A fallen migrant, a rodent
frozen at footsteps? Or, sigh relief, just a crumpled
leaf. Of a sudden honks tumble from on high, honk honk
honk, as if breaking entrance to that other sky, of light,
of place where suns set so much later. The V passes in a blink,
itself only a denser gray of wavering air, vanishes long
before the shattering calls. In the silence of their wake do you not hear
first the rustle of the unsnapping, the shedding,
the letting go, then don't you see it, the stupid concrete
mold made to bear our caprices as uniforms – witch's hat,
Easter basket and flowery dress, et cetera – to fit our seasons?
Look, can you see in our obscure below,
how it stretches stone wings, unwinds long neck, from a puddle
of premature orange and black clothes,
takes off

*In American Midwestern suburbs, some people decorate their porches with cement geese that they costume according to holidays.

-- Anca Vlasopolos

To My Father

Where Herekino jumps up
pushing away from blades
of time and purpose
you still fly your Tiger Moth

along the swamps
wearing your sheepskin-lined
leather flying jacket, lupine grin
grimacing from clouds
like this rainbow. For moments
volcanoes erupt, drought in June
and a fertile sea. Days break
into omens; we, heritage seeds
ignore our polished acquisitions
amongst babies boomed by rhetoric, fed
bile and lemons light as leaves. Faith
in pleasure put whips in our work
on the purple fever mesa, tumours shrunken
like heads. Your passion, ecstatic
and personal, terrified us, nights
in denial alienated from life.
We wanted to love, applauded
judges set loose within the edifice
and brought to ground in the light
shone by builders of departure ramps,
a million attempts at liberation
equalling nothing, no measure of the past.

From then until now your flying helmet
turns away towards your own infinity;
for me though nothing is infinite
and I misplaced your rank and number
somewhere between love and approval
so when I try to hear you – your arrival

lights dim flickers on pinned-up sheets –
to listen to you from this stalled step
separated from the potent skies
above my home-town honeysuckle,
to hear again what once I would not comprehend
such sweet dishonesty – to hear you
(pigeons and trees, even wind hushes to listen)
fly overhead with your tuneless song
trailing a veil behind you
be true, be true, be true
like everything else, death
dwindles, insipid and weak.

-- Mercedes Webb-Pullman

Why the Window Washer Reads Poetry
for Michael, who carried poems in his work shirt pocket

He lowers himself
on a seat they call a cradle, rocking
in harnesses strung long-armed
from the roof.

Swiping windows clean
he spends his day
outside looking in.

Mirrors refract light into his eyes
telescopes point down
photographs face away,
layers of dust
unifying everything.

Tethered and counterbalanced
these sky janitors hang,
names stitched on blue shirts
for birds to read.
Squeegees in hand they
arc lightly back and forth across
the building's eyes
descend a floor, dance again.

While the crew catches up
he pauses, takes a slim volume from his pocket
and balancing there,
36 stories above the street,
reads a poem or two
in which the reader is invariably placed
inside
looking out.

-- Laura Grace Weldon

So Soon

I'm reminded of an egg's
brief perfection.
What grows within
must crack what contains it.

At seventeen
you squint at farther horizons
bits of childhood still
in your hair, your walk, your laugh.

Behind you
this place we fashioned
each twig bent to nestle you
just so, will ever after be
changed by your flight.

-- Laura Grace Weldon

Above All Else

>Sullen bird, you are swollen with memories,
>caked with too much earth; come back.
>>Lose flight.
>>Set yourself on fire along with the alphabet.
>Build stars out of the oil dripping from your wings;
>go soft, touch the moon.
>>Blow the fire inward.
>>Slip into the tarnished melt of light.
>Take flight; you are weightless, you are the word.
>Sing the dark above all else. Now bolt.

>>*-- Sara Williams*

Return Flight

The lake had been invaded by purple loosestrife.
It was "choking out" other foliage and open water areas,
changing the area into an unwelcoming place
for nesting Black terns.
The rangers had to add their lack of sighting
onto the endangered list.

But after an effort to clean the lake,
the Black terns were back –
assembling their nests in small, loose settlements
using floating masses of dead vegetation.

Now, in breeding season,
their plumage darkens around the head and chest,
its gray wings are distinctive in the healing sky.

You cannot confuse it with the other birds
landing around the lake.

His wife observes through binoculars
as they draw straight lines in flight
before wavering into a dive. She gasps
with the suddenness of strike and catch.

She asks, *why don't you dive into me
that way anymore? Why don't you
change color when ready to mate?*

Too often, his fishing line is empty.
Too often, he is absent in sightings.
His answers are floating masses of dead vegetation
on the stillness of a lake,
his marriage is marked on the endangered list.

It is too late for a return flight, he wonders,
into astonishment? His hair darkening
as he nears into her peripheral vision
becoming a surprise of strike-and-catch.

        -- Martin Willitts, Jr.

Finding the Blue Huron

The Great Huron invented stillness,
and practiced yoga on one leg with the cranes.

It wore white morning light, like a robe.

It knew the patterns of fish;
the purpose of waiting to see
what happens next;
the patience of finding
what you need
and when to get it.

My wife bending her neck in blue reading light,
studies the same intense stillness
as if her life depended upon it.

I balance on one leg finding what I need
and not wanting to disturb it.

-- Martin Willitts, Jr.

Sidemen or Birds on the Same Wave Length Branch

1.   *The music, man, the music*

the twelve tones of a chromatic scale
are the twelve step program of AA.
A scale can lead melodically to any key,
breaking and entering like a thief
into some constrictions
of simpler jazz soloing –

the symmetry of equally placed notes
are endless servings of food,
major and minor keys
are skeleton keys or pick locks,
the ascending and descending scales
is an elevator
unable to make up its mind.

It is the difference between an improviser
and an amateur, or birds in flight
and flightless birds. One is inspired;
the other would not know cool
if locked in a deep-freezer.

2.   John Birks "Dizzy" Gillespie

adding layers of harmonic complexity,
bricks or sashaying hips. His black beret
for that extra sense of class in a no-class club.
Horn-rimmed glasses full of city blares,
scat singing. His bent horn pounded on
some anvil or sat on, according to his own legend.
Pouched cheeks. Light-hearted sounds
of surprise. An avalanche of notes
unendingly diverse as a city itself, break-

neck flourishes chased by pauses
like horses to the finish line.

He would make gigantic interval jumps,
tossing anvils of laws against musical notations,
blaring immensely intense high notes,
slurs and smears and affronts
to classical tastes. That bent horn
was an ostrich at rest. Or the angle of sound.

3.   Maxwell Lemuel "Max" Roach

Percussion is end of discussion.
Insert African accents snare drum.
Crash cymbal car crash or face slap.
Capture the components of the moment
in a trap set. Tap, tap, a blind man
finding his way through density of forests
flexing muscular sounds. Keep time,
rhythms of pigeons taking street noises,
rasps of babies, bottled-up lust,
sizzles of hot dogs, smoke forming hips,
ducking thrown beer bottle, snap
twigs, lush oasis of palm trees and camels
folding down knees into burning sand,
flamingoes of sunsets – it all goes in.

4.   Earl Rudolph "Bud" Powell

A piano is the call to wake. Large hands
find the Righteousness and His solos,
visualized in emulation of and opposition with,
what had transpired between silence,

a prayer being answered
and not necessarily matching the question –

frequent arpeggios
punctuating keys,
progressive-sounding, harmonic series
in unexpected ways.
Mistake? Not so.

Audacious passages at faster tempo,
heat spikes, clicking typewriter keyboards,
high heels on spasmodic sidewalks.

5.   Charles Mingus Jr. says

Focus on improvisation.
Make things happen. Focus
on the carotid artery. From the belly,
pregnant with sounds, not
from the head, comes a rumble,
an approaching train.
It is from the bass – deepness
of cave and birth-moans. Blend
and bend, rub and thump.

Pay attention:

each band member should interact
with the group,
should be how whiskey and ginger ale mix,
not like gunpowder
and switchblades.

Look at creation.
Music should be that explosive.
It should be the same as observing
both the proficiency of the available musicians,
as well as their personalities.

Me,
I am the angry man of Jazz.

Take Bird for example:

He plays off the sheets
where music is not
and makes them happen –

like a cement mixer
giving birth to sparrows,

or shoe polish
making fierce solos,

or winged pianos,
or flights of stairs into hibernation,

or convoluted, clutters of cardinals,
unwashed minds of alcoholics,
tubular angst from potholes and potheads,
fulcrums of steel,

pylons taunt ribcages,
mangled, meshed, thrashed wheat,
any throw-back to old music
or flashes out-of-nowhere music,
sleet or pebbles,
downpours of sunshine
so cold
it bakes eggs.

6.   Feeling

Play what you feel

If you feel like
you been run over by a truck
or fallen down circular stairs
or wrung through a wringer
or splashed against a wall
into Jackson Pollack paint

or rubbed the wrong way
creating static electricity
or rubbed out or wearing rubbers
and I don't mean goulashes
or hit by a rubber truncheon
or running against the wind
or against the grain or following
myopic dreams or lost your way
on a one way street of no desire
or your body is going many directions
or lost its place or forgot loss
or remember flavors that don't exist
or fashions itself
on whatever is fashionable at the moment
or flips like eggs at impulse
or believes life revolves like a record
or reloads life with emphatic bullets
or takes a woman on a date
forgetting her name
when it is written on your sleeve,
or waking up at the wrong address
with someone you don't know
with no excuses,

then
play what you feel.

-- Martin Willitts, Jr.

The Weaver Bird Colony

Since Fatima had discovered the weaver bird colony, she had become more and more fascinated by these birds: how the males hung upside down under the cute woven nests and fluttered their wings and squawked while the females hopped from branch to branch with their heads on one side as if to say: "I like the way that one dances" before joining their chosen mate to make a home together.

Fatima sighed, if only it were that simple at the school discos.

-- Juliet Wilson

Together We Watch

Every dusk I stay with her
awhile, offer some semblance
of comraderie. How feeble
I must seem, unable to dive

deep and impale a bream—
no stiletto beak, no poking beneath
spatterdock leaves for sunfish and bass,
no wings to fly up to the tip

of a willow thicket and keep watch
over Taylor Slough. If only I knew
why she stayed behind.
Together we watch two alligators

roll and rumble, listen
to their mating bellows, then
watch one float away log-like
to the Pond apples. Together—

anhinga clinging with stubby webbed
feet to willow branch, one human leaning
on boardwalk railing—we watch
Great egrets fly over, thunder

clouds gather. When I whisper,
I'm poised to fly, if I just had wings . . .
she doesn't stir. But I've a hunch
she comprehends.

-- Diana Woodcock

Migrations

Contemplating wings,
I think of miraculous
mysterious migrations,
of species and ecosystems
in jeopardy: butterflies;

hummingbirds; snow geese;
bats—four million from Mexico
to Texas and back each year—
controlling insects, dispersing seeds.
Tens of millions of monarchs

flying central Mexico to as far north
as Canada —five generational waves,
the last returning to a place they've
never been two thousand miles away.
The five-foot Whooping crane

voyaging twenty-four hundred miles
from Canada's boreal forest to winter
along the Texas coast—prairies,
wetlands, floodplains what they need most
as they refuel and rest along the way.

Mulling over migration highways

endangered by new roads and houses,
shopping malls and suburban sprawl,
I awaken to the mystery, imagine
making such a journey year after year,

caught up in the sacred balance. Hear
the haunted honking of geese passing over
in their faultless V. See the sight

of thousands of monarchs alight on limbs
to rest until the next leg of their flight.

Envisioning wings, I find the door.
Spring, autumn passages.
Messages of hope, each lifting off,
each return. Who would not yearn
for wings and the migratory instinct?

If only one Rufous hummer arrives
in Misty Fiords, Alaska this summer
to feast on Salmon- and Blueberries,
it will be reason enough reason to not give up.

-- Diana Woodcock

The Late Blooming of Harriet Milne

Harriet, a slender and tallish woman elegantly attired in deep mourning, positioned herself in front of the mirror in and unpinned her hat.

'Fifteen years,' she observed to Emmie, her brother's pretty young wife, 'is a long time to be married. I am afraid I have grown rather used to it, and I cannot give the whole business up. Arthur had his faults, it is true, but now I find I miss him. I have placed an advertisement in the Oakleigh Gazetteer. I mean to marry again.'

Emmie's eyes widened and she blushed to the roots of her hair. Harriet's boldness was shocking but it was also exciting.

'You can't possibly mean it,' said Emmie.

'Oh, but I do.'

There was a stubborn line to Harriet's mouth and a certain pugnacity about the tilt of her chin.

Emmie and Bertie spent the evening in the parlour. Emmie sat with her head bowed over the delicate fabric of her embroidery where, from the startling, scarlet platform of a nodding, full-blown poppy, a blue and emerald butterfly seemed poised to take flight. As she counted threads, she thought about Harriet, recalling their earlier conversation. Then, without understanding why, she repeated it to Bertie.

After a time, Bertie ceased to bluster and recovered his composure.

My sister is quite mad,' he said. 'Arthur, God rest him, was a rough sort of chap but he took her warts and all. More to the point, he was the kind of man who could keep her in line; and, if things had come to the worst, he had the money to be able to look after her. Harriet has a wild streak, a dangerous kind of madness. More than once, as a younger woman, she had to be sent away.'

Emmie was shocked by his manner of speaking but she asked no more questions, resolving instead to raise the matter with her friend at the first opportunity.

She did not have long to wait. Harriet came calling the next morning. Her cheeks were flushed from the briskness of the walk and she was all over dewy and damp.

'Isn't the rain wonderful?' she said. Her brown eyes were shining and her hat was on askew as she fumbled with the buttons of her rain coat.

'Thank heavens Bertie's out,' observed Emmie, unsettled by her sister-in-law's excitement. She took the proffered coat and hung it on a hook.

'Oh, Emmie, you won't believe what has happened.'

'In that case, we had better have tea. Come with me to the kitchen. Annie's gone to market. Bertie is demanding a pair of kippers for his tea.

Against the possibility of Bertie's return, they retired to Emmie's little sewing-room. It was a clutter of fabrics and unfinished projects but Emmie felt comfortable there. She even had permission to light a small fire.

'Now,' she said, 'tell me your news but, later, I have something to ask you. Shall I be Mother?'

Emmie lifted the pot.

Harriet's workman-like, nail-bitten fingers trembled as she lifted her teacup.

'I have received a reply to my advertisement,' she said. 'His name is Charles Thomas Ingle, a bachelor in his forties and a solicitor by profession, although, perhaps, not the very best sort.'

Emmie's brow furrowed but Harriet continued briskly. 'It's is an excellent opportunity and I mean to have him if I can.'

'What will Bertie say?' gasped Emmie, impressed by this show of independence

'I don't care what he says. May I have another cup of tea?'

Harriet agreed to show Emmie the letter but wouldn't permit her to read it. Written on superior cream-coloured paper, it was the work of a confident hand.

'Why can't I read it? I could help you decide.'

'Parts of it are racy,' replied Harriet, colouring. 'Anyway, I don't *need* any help.'

Harriet Milne and Charles Thomas Ingle were married a fortnight later. Harriet was radiant in dove grey and Emmie wound pink rosebuds in her hair. Bertie was there, too, very red in the face in the company of a pasty-faced policeman. When the officer explained there was nothing he could do Bertie raged and fumed.

Emmie, in a smart navy suit, was there as Harriet's witness. She stood on the steps of the Registry Office and waved her sister-in-law off. She never did discover whether Harriet was mad or if Bertie was just being spiteful. The morning after Harriet's wedding, Emmie packed her bags and left.

-- Abigail Wyatt

A Light of Their Own

Pale yellow butterflies,
wings like worn cloth,
aloft,
in a light
of their own,
a light made candescent
by misguided
dreams,
slights dragged
so deeply into spirit
they bruise the flesh,
small fears worried
into large, heavy knots.
They should be fluttering
above the aster and the bluestem,
lightly and unburdened.
But we find them in raftered
shadow,
swinging,
wings flattened,
light doused,
and even more pale.

Ah, why not wish
for a world gone mute?
Butterflies wounded,
dead,
and I ask for this.

-- Dana Yost

September 29, Altitude 30,000 Feet

Low mountains cloaked with dark conifers
and aspens going gold that climb them

Anything green is irrigated except
offal run-off from a spent copper mine

We suffer from headwaters erosion
Our dreams are mauvaise terres

compromised verb forms that end in –ing
tired like Kansas from sloping uphill to the west

The plane's wing kept blocking from view
what we had imagined we wanted to see.

If a nurse asks me to rate my level of pain
I'll ask: "Are we flying United in Economy?"

-- Ed Zahniser

What I Learned from the Flying Wings

different-coloured feathers, | | castrated words | |,
eyes scrolling up & down, plucked feathers
become transplanted onto your mind, & mess
the dancefloor of your dreams, dream is a
synonym of flight, flight is a transgression
against a status quo, & the words stagnate in
the nest, all of a sudden, the nestlings begin
chirruping, & the nest shakes, words start flying
in a shake, & begin to taste like a rainbow,
Wings, a plethora of dreams, & the pure blood
of freedom [seminal] always percolates the
flying wings, bestowing fecundity on the
castrated words,   & the revolution
won't succeed unless the flying wings copulate
w/ the rainbow.

-- Ali Znaidi

From The Editors

Poised In Flight

Egret rests on restraining rope
of pretentious yacht. Wings back,
head raised in mockery of modern
ostentation. Slyly scanning dock
for audience, it releases lone cry
of contempt(?) before launching
the perfect example of smooth
sailing.

-- A.J. Huffman

The Fire Catches

my skin in its teeth, but does not
burn. Instead, it dances down
my back, teaching my pores
the meaning of percussion until I am
alight in smokeless communication.
A moving signal of free
flowing. Thought: Do I care
if the rain puts me out?

-- A.J. Huffman

Of Perch and Purpose

The winter owl waits in perfect
immobilization, frozen as its name's
implications. Only eyes blink
occasionally to clear frosted
view. In the distance, a whisker,
a flick, hare's
tail barely visible,
fur against snow. White on white still
reads red. Target in line. Launch.
Claws capture quickly. A call of
triumph echoes
as it disappears into sky, sparing
our minds the memory of aftermath.

-- A.J. Huffman

From Balloon This Eruption

           of memories flow, electric-
al impulses traveling down thin-ribboned
strings into my closed fist, grasped tightly;

           of parks in summer, echoing
with laughter and lint from ground-covering
blankets. Plaid print, sun tickling back
of necks and interlocked fingers;

           of red, not quite the same
vibrant shade as inflated rubber orb, hair
tangling in the wind resistance created by absence
of convertible's top;

           of candles' flickering flames,
relighting themselves after attempt to blow
them out. Iced roses and silly animated cards
mark passage of another year;

           of release, the desire to not close
the circle so completely, to let streamers slip
from cracks, slide from fingers, to let everything
held fly
        free.

                    -- A.J. Huffman

Have a Happy Period

I will never forget the first time
I saw one. *They have wings*,
the commercial trilled. As if
that explained everything. A visual
of it seeming to wait, in mock embrace,
for the spreading blue
liquid that I, personally, never secreted.

I pulled one from the package, wrapped
like the tiny little gift it was not,
unfolded it. It looked like an albino
blueprint for an airplane. I prayed
it would carry "the curse" away with it.
It never did. It just had two additional
glue tabs to cling to my panties at odd
angles, irritating my skin. *It has wings,*
I thought as I adjusted it into place,
wondering if it was sad to be stuck
in a damp and windless place.

-- A.J. Huffman

Footless Pigeons

are a figment of my imagination, comment
on the fallible nature of memory, subjective,
the tendency to color the past more vivid, like eyes
of blue dogs. Goo on rooftops is real
enough but the birds die there, or later
bleed to death from the loss.
No one-footed pigeons hopped
around Regents, skirting my bench
for crumbs of a Safeway
loaf of 25p bread. Yet I remember them
as vividly as once upon a time,
as real as two
twenty-three-year-old writers
married till death did them part,
taking notes on hues of abstraction
in search of metaphor, for which a footless
carrier in flight would have been perfect.

-- April Salzano

Layover

I sealed my own fate by rescuing you. Snowstorm,
airport, connection cancelled.
They wanted to re-route you to D.C. instead
of New Jersey for a layover to London. At home,
I spent 48 hours on the phone with airline
customer service. You stayed in the airport
and waited for the next nonstop to Heathrow.
The purpose: a book fair, find an agent, maybe
get some exposure for the novel you had finally
finished, and detox alone, a last-ditch
effort to save yourself. If you had never
gotten on that plane, the chain
of events would have been broken, dominoes
withstanding the threat of a fall. By touch-
down, 2 days later, you were shaking
with withdrawal, cloudy, lost and anything but
straight. It took less than a few hours to find
your first target on the subway. She got away.
The second had more interest, got you high
with heroine from a hooker and coke from her mother,
or maybe that was the second trip to London,
four months later. The purpose: finish
another novel, find an agent, maybe get some
exposure, and detox alone. For real this time.
Lies you told me, our children, yourself
just to see her again.
That flight went more smoothly, without
unexpected delay. You were a metal bird scraping
the sky for scraps of a life. Everything
is easier in May. Marriages fall apart
in winter when belongings thrown in the yard
are much harder to find.

-- April Salzano

Summoning Seagulls

We have just left the doctor's office.
I am sufficiently belittled for not
having taken you to the dentist
by age 7. I tally one more for autism.
You are significantly
relieved at having survived
tongue depressor, throat swab,
thermometer. In the parking lot
we create a frenzy of beating wings
with leftover French fries. Seagulls,
their name a misnomer, ride vertical
air currents, swoop and scoop
wasted food, whole generations
who have probably never seen the sea,
born of parking lot parents, scavenging
easy meals of litter. You know
something of displacement and mirage,
how the world can be a confusing
place. You think you are at the ocean,
but it's only pavement.

You create symbiosis,
bite the ends off each fry, toss the middle
from the open car door, watch
the bird-battle. Only one will emerge
and carry the reward away.
The others pace the asphalt as if
it were sand. As long as they don't
get too close, you will keep
laughing. As long as you keep
throwing fries, they will keep
waiting. I can't get to my camera

in time, but try to memorize your smile
before you fly back to sea.

-- April Salzano

Flying South

Today the snow is a deep challenge
covering landmarks of the yard.
The long-vacant birdbath, the concentric circles
of grass killed by the inflatable swimming pool,
erased. The cardinal's blood red is the only contrast
at the feeder. Yesterday was your birthday.
I pretend I know the climate eight hours south
from where you sent me a picture of you
standing with your children. The daughter
who was not even born when we met is even
with your shoulder and wears your face.
Your son is a teenager who tries
to resist the cost of a smile. As I watch the cold
vapor of breath leave my body,
I cannot remember your street
address from fifteen years ago. I am not sure
why it matters, but I try through the length
of a cigarette and come up with nothing.
Such things, small tags of concrete
serve as my signposts, relics to guide me
through the distance imposed by time,
circumstance. I know as we age another year,
another winter, that I will get lost in this snow
and never find my way south.

-- April Salzano

Auto Pilot

A mirror broken, reflection
of insults hanging in the air like glass.
Who knows why
we were fighting, but it felt
as if a month-long marriage was about
to die. At 23, we thought we knew something
of domestic disturbance and dramatic exit.
I hurled myself on the mattress that served
as our borrowed bed in a rented 2nd floor, pounding
the pillow in lament. Whatever
you had done, it was serious, that much
was certain. In the hour you were gone,
I had planned our divorce and considered packing
your clothes. By the time I heard you calling
my name under the window, sadness
had given way to low boiling anger.
You directed me to the sky,
overpopulated with hot air
balloons. A supernova of primary-colored
polyester punctuated the clear blue.
Riding the wind, the lighting of our metaphor
filled every space of horizon.
We had no choice but to make up.

-- *April Salzano*

Author Bios

Kenton Adler is a writer and musician living Batesville, AR. Kenton was born in Arkansas, raised in Colorado and moved back to Arkansas in 1992. Adler works for the Development office of Lyon College by day. He is the author of a young adult novel, The Silver Pipes of Tir nan Og, An Alligator In Your Yard, and a number of poems. Ken plays guitar and has written and recorded a number of songs. He is also a bagpiper with the Lyon College Pipe Band. He is married to Nancy Love.

Joe Amaral is a paramedic who spends most of his time spelunking around the California central coast. His poetry and short stories have appeared in awesome places like *A Handful of Dust, amphibi.us, Certain Circuits, Diverse Voices Quarterly, Kind of a Hurricane Press, RED OCHRE LiT, Tolosa Press,* and *Underground Voices*. He also has pieces published internationally via *Decanto Magazine, Litro*, and *Taj Mahal Review*.

Linda Bearss has published a variety of poetry as well as articles on the writings of Theodore Roethke and Paul Laurence Dunbar. Ms. Bearss is a poet/writer/teacher, who instructs high school and college students in literature and composition. She has earned two master degrees in English language and literature and continues to keep abreast of contemporary renovations in both fields. Ms. Bearss is also a member of the National Writing Project, Society for the Study of Midwestern Literature, and Academy of American Poets.

Alan Britt most recently had his interview at The Library of Congress for *The Poet and the Poem* air on Pacifica Radio January 2013. His interview with *Minnesota Review* is up at. He read poems at the World Trade Center/Tribute WTC Visitor Center in Manhattan/NYC, April 2012 and at the Maysles

Cinema in Harlem/NYC, February 2013. His latest books are *Alone with the Terrible Universe* (2011), *Greatest Hits* (2010), *Hurricane* (2010), *Vegetable Love* (2009), *Vermilion* (2006), *Infinite Days* (2003), *Amnesia Tango* (1998) and *Bodies of Lightning* (1995). He is Poetry Editor for the We Are You Project International (www.weareyouproject.org) and Book Review Editor for *Ragazine* (http://ragazine.cc/). He teaches Creative Writing at Towson University.

Terry Brix, a "green" chemical engineer, divides his time among Blue River, Oregon; Bozeman, Montana; Scandinavia; and China. Inspired by his travels, a collection of his poetry *Chiseled from the Heart* was published in 2000 by Vigeland Museum, Norway. His poetry has appeared in, among others, *Concho River Review, The Evansville Review, Fireweed, Curbside Review, Rattlesnake Review, The Antioch Review* and *North American Review*. He is currently working on a new collection of poems written during his travels and a month-long writer's fellowship residency at Playa. www.terrybrix.com

Diana Brodie, whose first collection, Giotto's Circle, will be published in the summer, 2013 by Poetry Salzburg, has had many publications in journals such as *Agenda, Rialto, Obsessed with Pipework, Off the Coast*, and her work has appeared in several anthologies including *Entering the Tapestry* and *The Iron Book of Humorous Verse*. Born in New Zealand, she now lives in Cambridge, UK.

Michael H. Brownstein has been widely published throughout the small and literary presses. His work has appeared in *The Café Review, American Letters and Commentary, Skidrow Penthouse, Xavier Review, Hotel Amerika, Free Lunch, Meridian Anthology*

of Contemporary Poetry, The Pacific Review, Poetrysuperhighway.com and others. In addition, he has nine poetry chapbooks including *The Shooting Gallery* (Samidat Press, 1987), *Poems from the Body Bag* (Ommation Press, 1988), *A Period of Trees* (Snark Press, 2004), *What Stone Is* (Fractal Edge Press, 2005), and *I Was a Teacher Once* (Ten Page Press, 2011). He is the editor of *First Poems from Viet Nam* (2011).

Dorothy Burgess is a member of Southport Writers' Circle. She has had a number of poems published.

Janet Butler relocated to the Bay Area in 2005 after many years in central Italy. She teaches ESL Test Prep in San Francisco and lives in Alameda with Fulmi, a lovely Spaniel mix she rescued in Italy and brought back with her. Some current or forthcoming publications are Constellations, The Tipton Poetry Journal, Floodwall, Ascent Aspirations, and Red Ochre Lit. "Searching for Eden" was published in early 2012 by Finishing Line Press, "Upheaval" was recently selected as one of three winning chapbooks in the Red Ochre Press 2012 Chapbook Contest.

Miki Byrne is the author of two poetry collections. She has had work included in over 120 poetry magazines and anthologies. She has won prizes for her poetry and has read on both Radio and TV and judged poetry competitions. She has a BA (Hons.) in 3D Design and a PGCE. Her new collection 'Flying Through Houses' will be available from Indigo Dreams Press in 2013. Miki is disabled and lives in Gloucestershire, England

Tiffany Chaney is a writer and artist based in North Carolina. Her work is featured in such publications as Thrush Poetry Journal, Pedestal Magazine, and Virginia Quarterly Review

(InstaPoetry Series). Her first poetry collection—Between Blue and Grey—won the Best in Poetry, 2013 Mother Vine Festival Award. She holds a B.A. in creative writing from Salem College. Visit www.tiffanychaney.com for more.

Esteban Colon is a Writer and Experiential Educator from the Chicago land area. He is one of the founding members of the Waiting 4 the Bus Poetry Collective, Co-hosts a poetry open mic, and a poetry showcase show. The Editor in Chief for *Exact Change Only*, he is the proud author of *Between Two Lines* and *Edgar Avenue*. His work has seen print in varied publications such as *Rhino*, *After Hours*, *CC&D Magazine*, and Outrider Press' Black and White Anthology Series, and others.

Susan Dale has had her poems and fiction published on *Eastown Fiction, Ken *Again, Hackwriters, Yesteryear Fiction, Feathered Flounder*, and *Penwood Review*. In 2007, she won the grand prize for poetry from Oneswan.

Cassandra Dallett occupies Oakland, CA. Cassandra writes of a counter culture childhood in Vermont and her ongoing adolescence in the San Francisco Bay Area. She has published in *Slip Stream, Sparkle and Blink, Hip Mama, Bleed Me A River, Criminal Class Review, Enizagam* among many others. Look for links and chapbooks on cassandradallett.com.

Jim Davis is is a graduate of Knox College and an MFA candidate at Northwestern University. Jim lives, writes, and paints in Chicago, where he edits the *North Chicago Review*. His work has appeared in *Seneca Review, Blue Mesa Review, Poetry Quarterly, Whitefish Review, The Café Review,* and *Contemporary American Voices*, in addition to winning the *Line Zero* Poetry Contest, *Eye on Life* Poetry Prize, multiple Editor's Choice awards, and a recent nomination for the *Best of the Net* Anthology.

R.C. Davis is a poet and writer/author of short fiction, who has been penning poetry and prose since his twelfth year of life. Initially inspired by Robert Frost and Mark Twain, he has a preference toward reading and writing Romantic Ballads. A globally thinking man and humanitarian with altruistic tendencies, he has traveled Europe, Ireland and the UK. His published works include *'The Light in the Window'* - Wapsi Almanac, Route 3 Press. *'Cane Pole Logic'* - Amber Waves of Grain, An anthology of short stories, *'Hodgepodge Style'* - Strange Cage Press of Iowa City, *'Murdering Box Elder'* along with *'Under the Eaves'* - Sackter House Publications, plus many more. R.C. resides in Iowa City, Iowa (a UNESCO city of literature) with his deaf dog Daisy.

Neil Ellman lives and writes in New Jersey. More than 600 of his poems, many of which are ekphrastic and based on works of modern and contemporary art, appear in numerous print and online journals, anthologies, broadsides and chapbooks throughout the world. He has been nominated twice for *Best of the Net*.

Alexis Rhone Fancher is a writer/photographer. Her latest chapbook is *Gidget Goes To The Ghetto*. Her "pillow book," *explicit,* came out in 2010. She studies with the poet, Jack Grapes, and is a member of his L.A. Poets & Writers Collective. Her work has been published or is forthcoming in *High Coupe, Mas Tequila Review, Gutter Eloquence* Magazine, *Cultural Weekly, Tell Your True Tale, Downer* Magazine, *Bare Hands Anthology,* Ireland, *The Sun* Magazine, *Spark Off Rose, The Poetry Juice Bar* and elsewhere. Her erotic thriller, <u>Annie's Sinful Nature</u>, awaits publication.

Mike Florian has been published in various on line and printed magazines. His work has been seen in Ascent Aspirations, The National Post and Bewildering Stories Magazine among others. Mike lives in North Vancouver, Canada.

Patricia L. Goodman is a widowed mother and grandmother, a graduate of Wells College with a degree in Biology and is a member of Phi Beta Kappa. Her career involved breeding and training horses with her orthodontist husband on their farm in Chadds Ford, PA. She has had poems published in *Aries, The Broadkill Review, Sugar Mule, Requiem Magazine, Jellyfish Whispers, Fox Chase Review, Mistletoe Madness* (Kind of a Hurricane Press)*On Our Own* (Silver Boomer Books) and forthcoming in *The Widow's Handbook*. Her first book and chapbook are being presented to publishers. She lives on the banks of the Red Clay Creek in Delaware, where she is surrounded by the natural world she loves.

Mavis Gulliver lives in the Inner Hebrides, Scotland. Her poetry stems from close observation of the landscape and wildlife around her. Many of her poems have appeared in poetry magazines such as Envoi, Iota and Poetry Scotland. They can also be found in anthologies - 'No Space But Their Own (Grey Hen - 2010), 'Shropshire Butterflies (Fairacre Press - 2011), 'These Islands, We Sing' (Polygon - 2011) and 'The Price of Gold' (Grey Hen - 2012). She is currently working on a collection of island poems; and a further collection about the slate islands, in collaboration with Jan Fortune of Cinnamon Press, is due to be published in 2014.

Nels Hanson graduated from UC Santa Cruz and the U of Montana and his fiction received the San Francisco Foundation's James D. Phelan Award. His stories have appeared in Antioch

Review, Texas Review, Black Warrior Review, Southeast Review, Montreal Review, and other journals. "Now the River's in You," in Ruminate Magazine, was nominated for a 2010 Pushcart Prize, and "No One Can Find Us," in Ray's Road Review, has been nominated for the 2012 Pushcart Prizes. Poems have appeared in Poetry Porch, Atticus Review, Red Booth Review, Meadowlands Review, Emerge Literary Review, Shot Glass, Language and Culture, Outside In Literary & Travel Magazine, Writer's Ink, Jellyfish Whispers, and other magazines.

Richard D. Hartwell is a retired middle school (remember, the hormonally-challenged?) English teacher living in Moreno Valley, California, with his wife of thirty-six years (poor soul, her, not him), their disabled daughter, one of their sons and his ex-wife and their two children, and eleven cats. Yes, eleven! He believes in the succinct, that the small becomes large; and, like the Transcendentalists and William Blake, that the instant contains eternity. Given his "druthers," if he's not writing poetry, Rick would rather still be tailing plywood in a mill in Oregon.

Art Heifetz teaches ESL to refugees in Richmond, Va. He has had over 60 poems published in 6 countries since June. A sampling of his work appears at polishedbrasspoems.com.

S.E.Ingraham pens poems from Edmonton, Alberta - Canada's northernmost provincial capital. She, along with an aging wolf/border-collie, plus the love of her life, try to stay out of trouble there, and in Italy, where she's been spending recent summers with a cadre of crypt-kickers (aka archaeological students). Recent work has appeared or will soon in: Pyrokinection, Shot Glass, Storm Cycle - The Best of 2012, Red Fez, Poetic Bloomings: The First Year, and Pay Attention: A River of Stones, among others. More of her work may be viewed here http://thepoet-tree-house.blogspot.ca/ or here http://leapinelephants.blogspot.ca/ or here http://seingrahamsays.wordpress.com/.

Ken L. Jones has been a professional writer for the past thirty plus years. He has published in practically every medium that a writer can appear in. Among his earliest and most noteworthy accomplishment was as a cartoonist of note whose scripts appeared in the titles of such major publishers as Disney Comics and Harvey Comics where he was a lead writer for The New Kids On The Block family of titles. In the last few years he has shifted his emphasis to writing speculative fiction and horror short stories as well as very well received poems of horror which have appeared many times in anthologies and online and which also resulted in his first solo book of poetry Bad Harvest and Other Poems which was released by Panic Press. In addition to all this he currently is constantly turning in new horror poems to George Wilhite's Long Intervals of Horrible Sanity blog which features regularly updated selections of his latest visions of terror. You can find it at the following link http://georgewilhite.blogspot.com/p/poetry-by-ken-l-jones.html.

Lora Keller began her career as a writer pounding out poems on her toy typewriter as a child in Kaukauna, Wisconsin. Since then, she has earned a Bachelor's degree in poetry and creative writing at the University of Wisconsin-Milwaukee. For 15 years, she was a scriptwriter and public relations executive in Milwaukee, New York and Kansas City. After that, she taught college business writing and composition for several years. For the last 15 years, she has owned and run three small businesses and turned again to writing poetry. Her work has been published in *Blast Furnace*, *The Shepherd Express* and the *Appleton Post-Crescent*.

Steve Klepetar whose work has appeared widely, has received several nominations for the Pushcart Prize and Best of the Net.

His latest chapbook is "My Father Had Another Eye," from Flutter Press.

Len Kuntz is a writer and editor at the online literary magazine Metazen. Over 700 of his stories appear in print and online. Len's story collection, "I'm Not Supposed To Be Here And Neither Are You" debuts from Aqueous Books next year. You can find him at lenkuntz.blogspot.com.

Heller Levinson lives in NYC where he studies animal behavior. He has published in numerous journals and magazines and his publication, *Smelling Mary* (Howling Dog Press, 2008), was nominated for both the Pulitzer Prize and the Griffin Prize. Black Widow Press published his *from stone this running* in 2012. Additionally, he is the originator of Hinge Theory.

pd lyons has been writing for a long time now and hopes to continue doing so for even longer. Work has appeared in many mags & zines throughout the world. Has two collections of poetry published by Lapwing Press Belfast. Please visit pdlyons blog for poetry publishing info and new releases: http://pdlyons.wordpress.com/.

Jacqueline Markowski has had her work appear in in numerous publications including *Cochlea/The Neovictorian, Permafrost Literary Journal, Camel Saloon, Pyrokinection* and *Jellyfish Whispers* and has been anthologized in "Backlit Barbell" and "Storm Cycle" (Kind of a Hurricane Press*)*. Her short stories have appeared in *PoundofFlash.com*. She was awarded first place in poetry at The Sandhills Writers Conference. She is currently working on a compilation of short stories and a collection of poetry.

Joe Massingham was born in the UK but has lived the second half of his life in Australia. Major employment has been as a Navy officer, university student from first degree to PhD, tutor, lecturer and Master of Wright College, University of New England, NSW. He has run his own business but because of cancer and heart problems he now spends time waiting to see medical practitioners, writing all sorts of things and smelling the roses. He has had 97 poems published in 2012, spread over 9 different countries. He has also worked as an academic editor and as a reviewer of Visual Arts, Poetry, Politcs and History works.

Janet McCann has had her poems published in *Kansas Quarterly, Parnassus, Nimrod, Sou'Wester, New York Quarterly, Tendril, Poetry Australia,* and others. She has won five chapbook contests, sponsored by Pudding Publications, Chimera Connections, Franciscan University Press, Plan B Press, and Sacramento Poetry Center. A 1989 NEA Creative Writing Fellowship winner, this crone poet has taught at Texas A & M University since 1969. Her most recent poetry collection: *Emily's Dress* (Pecan Grove, 2004).

Joan McNerney has been published in numerous literary magazines such as *Seven Circle Press, Dinner with the Muse, Blueline, Spectrum,* and three *Bright Spring Press Anthologies.* She has been nominated three times for *Best of the Net.* Four of her books have been published by fine small literary presses.

Karla Linn Merrifield, a seven-time Pushcart-Prize nominee and National Park Artist-in-Residence, has had more than 300 poems appear in dozens of journals and anthologies. She has nine books to her credit, the newest of which are *Lithic Scatter and Other Poems* (Mercury Heartlink) and *The Ice Decides: Poems of*

Antarctica (Finishing Line Press). Forthcoming from Salmon Poetry is *Athabaskan Fractal and Other Poems of the Far North*, and from FootHills Publishing, *Attaining Canopy: Amazon Poems*. Her *Godwit: Poems of Canada* (FootHills) received the 2009 Eiseman Award for Poetry and she recently received the Dr. Sherwin Howard Award for the best poetry published in *Weber - The Contemporary West* in 2012. She is assistant editor and poetry book reviewer for *The Centrifugal Eye (*www.centrifugaleye.com). Visit her blog, *Vagabond Poet*, at http://karlalinn.blogspot.com.

Bradley Morewood writes poetry in Tampa, Florida. His work recently appeared in Solo Novo, Red Ochre, Wild River Review, Pyrokinection, Jellyfish Whispers and Ubernothing.

Heidi Morrell has had her poetry published in *Big River Review, Unaureon, Cat's Magazine, Emerge Literary Journal, Outside In Literary & Travel Magazine, Big River Review,* and *St. James Newsletter.* Heidi also writes a bi-weekly column for Examiner.com - L.A. disability. go to: www.examiner.com/user-hbmorrell.

Lylanne Musselman is an award winning poet and artist. Her poems have appeared or are forthcoming in *Tipton Poetry Journal, Pank, Umbrella, The Prose-Poem Project, Bird's Eye reView,* and *The Rusty Nail* among others, and many anthologies. She is the author of three chapbooks: *Prickly Beer and Purple Panties* (Bacon Tree Press, 2007), A *Charm Bracelet For Cruising* (Winged City Press, 2009) and *Winged Graffiti* (Finishing Line Press, 2011). Presently, she teaches writing of all stripes at Terra Community College and is diligently working on a full length poetry memoir. Lylanne lives in Toledo, Ohio, with her three cats, Graham, Tink, and Fiyero.

Robbi Nester is the author of a chapbook, Balance (White Violet 2012). Her poems have been published in many journals, including *Broadsided, Poemeleon, Lummox, Inlandia, Jenny, Victorian Violet Press, Northern Liberties Review, Philadelphia Stories, Annapoorna, Spark 17 and 18, Qarrtsiluni, Floyd County Moonshine, and Caesura. Her essays, reviews, and interviews have been published in The Hollins Critic, Switchback, and in two anthologies: Easy to Love but Hard to Raise (DRT 2011) and Flashlight Memories (Silver Boomer Press 2011).*

ayaz daryl nielsen is a poet/editor/husband/father/army veteran/x-roughneck (as on oil rigs)/x-hospice nurse/editor of bear creek haiku (20+years/110+issues), resplendent homes for poems include Lilliput Review, Shemom (ed Peggy),Yellow Mama (ed Cindy), Shamrock (Irish Haiku Society, a most favorite online poetry pub), Lalitamba, also various anthologies/some awards (all deeply embraced), poetry ensembles include Concentric Penumbra's of the Heart, and, Tumbleweeds Still Tumbling, (both from the fierce poetry funhouse of ayaz daryl nielsen) beloved wife/poet Judith Partin-Nielsen, and! bearcreekhaiku.blogspot.com (translates as joie de vivre).

Alex Nodopaka originated in Ukraine-Russia in 1940. Studied at the Ecole des Beaux Arts, Casablanca, Morocco. Full time author, artist in the USA. His interests in the visual arts and literature are widely multi-cultural. However, he considers his past irrelevant as he seeks new reincarnations in IFC movies if only for the duration of a wink.

Selena Parrish lives in the mountains of NW Arkansas with her husband, artist Max Elbo, 3 cats & an infinite number of grey tree frogs. She is currently at work on "Do Do Rana Rana", a multimedia synopsis of tree frog song & habitat.

Winston H. Plowes writes his words with two cats on a narrowboat on England's inland waterways. His compositions have been widely published, hopefully making people pause and ponder the magical details of life.

PratimaBalabhadrapathruni is a poet, writer and artist who lives in Singapore.

Ben Rasnic is a native of Jonesville, a small rural town in Southwest Virginia with a population <1000. His poems have been published in *A Small Good Magazine, Bird's Eye reView, The Camel Review, Camroc Press Review, Flutter Magazine, Gutter Eloquence, The Orange Room Review, Right Hand Pointing, The Rusty Truck, Short, Fast and Deadly, Subliminal Interiors, Victorian Velvet Press* and numerous other print and online journals. He is also the author of two collections of poetry, "Artifacts and Legends" from Aldrich Press and "Puppet: Poems by Ben Rasnic" from Alabaster Leaves Publishing. A Pushcart Prize nominee in 2011, Rasnic still considers as his greatest literary achievement, electing to publish two short poems by Yusef Komunyakaa while serving as editor of his college literary magazine, Jimson Weed, in 1978—16 years before Komunyakaa received the Pulitzer Prize for Poetry. Ben currently resides in Bowie, Maryland.

henry 7. reneau, jr. has been published in various journals/anthologies, among them, *Nameless Magazine; Subliminal Interiors Literary Arts Magazine; The Chaffey Review; The View From Here; FOLLY Magazine; Entering; Tule Review; BlazeVOX; Black Heart Magazine; Suisun Valley Review;* and *Tidal Basin Review*. He has also self-published a chapbook entitled 13hirteen Levels of Resistance. His favorite things are Rottweilers, poetry relevant to a concealed, but actual, reality, his "fixie," and Ben & Jerry's New York Super Fudge Chunk.

Sy Roth comes riding in and then canters out. Oftentimes, the head is bowed by reality; other times, he is proud to have said something noteworthy. Retired after forty-two years as teacher/school administrator, he now resides in Mount Sinai. He spends his time writing and playing his guitar. He has published in many online publications such as *Mel BraKe Press, Larks Fiction Magazine, Exercise Bowler, Otoliths, BlogNostics, Every Day Poets, brief, The Weekenders, The Squawk Back, Bareback Magazine,* and many others. One of his poems, *Forsaken Man,* was selected for Best of 2012 poems in *Storm Cycle.* Also selected Poet of the Month in Poetry Super Highway, September 2012. His work was read at Palimpsest Poetry Festival in December 2012. He was named Poet of the Month for the month of February in BlogNostics.

Walter Ruhlmann works as an English teacher, edits mgversion2>datura and runs mgv2>publishing. Walter is the author of several poetry chapbooks and e-books in French and English and has published poetry, fiction and non-fiction in various printed and electronic publications world wide. Nominated for Pushcart Prize once. His latest collection Maore was published by Lapwing Publications, Belfast, 2013. His blog can be found at: http://http://thenightorchid.blogspot.fr/.

Elizabeth Schultz lives in Lawrence, Kansas, following retirement from the English Department of the University of Kansas, where she was Chancellor's Club Teaching Professor. She remains committed to writing about the people and the places she loves in academic essays, nature essays, and poems. These include Herman Melville, her mother, and her friends, the Kansas wetlands and prairies, Michigan's Higgins Lake, Japan, where she lived for six years, oceans everywhere. She has published several books, and her scholarly and creative work appears in numerous journals and reviews.

Lance Sheridan and **Barbara Sutton** began writing poetry together in January of 2013. Having penned almost a dozen poems in visual freestyle, eight of those have been accepted into numerous journals. What other poets are saying about their writing, "you send the reader on a journey through his own soul;" "symbolically thought provoking"; "the imagery is amazing;" and, "this is a sort of writing which deliberately flouts grammatical structure and any form of restriction. It is not words. It is more music you relax to, curl up listening with an abstract ear." All of their writings are in Visual Freestyle Works® 'We sift the human storm, the life storm, through the dust and debris of their souls, animating it into thoughts and words. And then we write, not guessing where it might go, exhaling our last breath toward the light.'

Carol Smallwood co-edited *Women on Poetry: Writing, Revising, Publishing and Teaching* (McFarland, 2012) on the list of Best Books for Writers by *Poets & Writers Magazine*; *Women Writing on Family: Tips on Writing, Teaching and Publishing* (Key Publishing House, 2012); *Compartments: Poems on Nature, Femininity, and Other Realms* (Anaphora Literary Press, 2011) received a Pushcart nomination. Carol has founded, supports humane societies.

Edward W. L. Smith is an emeritus professor of psychology now devoting much of his time to writing poetry and mysteries. The muses often beckon him as he walks on the beach or sits gazing at the marsh at his half-time home on a small coastal island. In response to these calls, he writes, paints, or takes photographs, depending on which muse speaks most appealingly.

Shelby Stephenson lives near Benson, North Carolina. He has a recent chapbook, *Play My Music Anyhow* (Finishing Line Press, 2013.

John Swain lives in Louisville, Kentucky. Crisis Chronicles Press published his most recent chapbook, *White Vases*.

Susan Tepper is the author of three published books of fiction and a chapbook of poetry. Her most recent title *From the Umberplatzen* (Wilderness House Press, 2012) is a novel in flash. Her novel *What May Have Been* (Cervena Barva Press, 2010) was co-authored with Gary Percesepe and nominated for a Pulitzer Prize. www.susantepper.com.

Anca Vlasopolos published the award-winning novel *The New Bedford Samurai*, the award-winning memoir *No Return Address: A Memoir of Displacement*, two collections of poems, *Walking Toward Solstice* and *Penguins in a Warming World*, three poetry chapbooks, a detective novel, *Missing Members*, and over two hundred poems and short stories. She was nominated several times for the Pushcart Award in poetry and fiction. She is associate editor of Corridors Magazine.

Mercedes Webb-Pullman graduated from the International Institute of Modern Letters, Victoria University Wellington New Zealand with her MA in Creative Writing 2011. Her work has appeared in many online journals and collections, eBooks and in print. She lives on the Kapiti Coast, reads at open mic sessions there and in the city, and works for Lazarus Media LLC as Assistant Editor, Pacific, and Editor-in-Chief, DM du Jour.

Laura Grace Weldon is a writer, editor, and occasionally useful farm wench. She lives with her family on Bit of Earth Farm where they raise cows, chickens, bees, and the occasional ruckus. She's the author of *Free Range Learning*. Recent poems have been published in *Christian Science Monitor, The Shine Journal, Atlanta Review, Halfway Down the Stairs, Mannequin Envy,* and *Dirty Napkin*. She also twirls ideas around on her blog http://lauragraceweldon.com/blog-2/.

Sara Williams resides in Ypsilanti, Michigan. An avid reader, writer, and teacher of poetry, she works as a creative writing lecturer at Eastern Michigan University and Writer-in-Residence with InsideOut Literary Arts Program in Detroit. Work is forthcoming from *Rufous City Review* and *Eunoia Review*.

Martin Willitts, Jr. retired as a MLS Senior Librarian in upstate New York. His forthcoming poetry books include "*Waiting For The Day To Open Its Wings*" (UNBOUND Content, 2013), "*Art Is the Impression of an Artist*" (Edgar and Lenore's Publishing House, 2013), "*City Of Tents*" (Crisis Chronicles Press, 2013), "*A Is for Aorta*" (Seven Circles Press, e-book, 2013), "Swimming *In the Ladle of Stars*" (Kattywompus Press, 2013), "*Late All Night Sessions with Charlie "the Bird" Parker and the Members of Birdland, in Take-Three*" (A Kind Of a Hurricane Press, ebook, 2013) and he is the winner of the inaugural Wild Earth Poetry Contest for his full length collection "*Searching For What Is Not There*" (Hiraeth Press, 2013).

Juliet Wilson is an Edinburgh based writer, adult education tutor and conservation volunteer. She blogs at *Crafty Green Poet* (http://craftygreenpoet.blogspot.com) and edits the poetry journal *Bolts of Silk* (http://boltsofsilk.blogspot.com). Her poetry pamphlet *Unthinkable Skies* was published in 2010.

Diana Woodcock who had her first full-length collection, *Swaying on the Elephant's Shoulder* nominated for a Kate Tufts Discovery Award, won the 2010 Vernice Quebodeaux International Poetry Prize for Women and was published by Little Red Tree Publishing in 2011. Her forthcoming chapbook, *Tamed by the Desert,* was a finalist in Finishing Line Press's 2012 Open Chapbook Competition. Her other chapbooks are *In the Shade of the Sidra Tree* (Finishing Line Press), *Mandala* (Foothills Publishing), and *Travels of a Gwai Lo*—the title poem of which was nominated for a Pushcart Prize. She has been teaching at Virginia Commonwealth University in Qatar since 2004. Prior to that, she lived and worked in Tibet, Macau and Thailand.

Abigail Wyatt was born an Essex girl but has lived most of her adult life in Cornwall. Since 2008, her poetry and short fiction, have been published in more than seventy outlets including a number of poetry and prose anthologies. She is a founding member of the Red River Poetry Collective and one of the editors of Poetry24. Once a teacher of English, Abigail now works part-time in a café and devotes as much time as possible to her writing.

Dana Yost was a state and national award-winning daily newspaper journalist for 29 years. He's the author of three published books: 2008's Grace, a collection of new poems; 2010's The Right Place, a collection of essays and poems; and 2012's A Higher Level: Southwest State Women's Tennis 1979-1992, a work of regional and sports history. He is a 2012 nominee for a Pushcart Prize in poetry. His poems have been published in such journals and magazines as *Pyrokinection, Jellyfish Whispers, New Plains Review, Empirical Magazine, South Dakota Magazine, Bare Root Review, Awakenings Review, Open Minds Quarterly, Relief,* and many others. He lives in Forest City, Iowa.

Ed Zahniser has had his poems appear in over 100 literary magazines in the U.S. and U.K.; eight anthologies; three books, *Mall hopping with the Great I AM* (Somondoco Press, 2006), *The Way to Heron Mountain* (Night Tree Press, 1984), *A Calendar of Worship and Other Poems* (Plane Buckt Press, 1994); and three chapbooks, most recently *Slow Down and Live* (2011), a collaboration with artist/designer Heather Watson, the Studio Pernot and Tatlin, PDF under Zines at pernotandtatlin.com.

Ali Znaidi (b.1977) lives in Redeyef, Tunisia where he teaches English at Tunisian public secondary schools. He writes poetry and has an interest in literature, languages, and literary translations. His work has appeared in *The Camel Saloon, Otoliths, The Tower Journal, streetcake, The Rusty Nail, Yes,Poetry, Shot Glass Journal, Ink Sweat and Tears, Mad Swirl, Unlikely Stories: Episode IV, Red Fez, Carcinogenic Poetry, Stride Magazine,* and other ezines. His debut poetry chapbook *Experimental Ruminations* was published in September 2012 by Fowlpox Press (Canada). He also writes flash fiction for the Six Sentence Social Network—http://sixsentences.ning.com/profile/AliZnaidi.

About The Editors

A.J. Huffman is a poet and freelance writer in Daytona Beach, Florida. She has previously published six collections of poetry all available on Amazon.com. She has also published her work in numerous national and international literary journals. Most recently, she has accepted the position as editor for six online poetry journals for Kind of a Hurricane Press (www.kindofahurricanepress.com).

April Salzano teaches college writing in Pennsylvania and is working on her first (several) poetry collections and an autobiographical work on raising a child with Autism. Her work has appeared in *Poetry Salzburg, Pyrokinection, Convergence, Ascent Aspiration, Deadsnakes, The Rainbow Rose* and other online and print journals and is forthcoming in *Inclement, Poetry Quarterly and Bluestem.*

Made in the USA
Lexington, KY
30 March 2013